Do As
I Say
(NOT AS I DO)

Do As I Say

(NOT AS I DO)

Profiles in
Liberal
Hypocrisy

Peter Schweizer

BROADWAY BOOKS   NEW YORK

PUBLISHED BY BROADWAY BOOKS

Copyright © 2005 by Peter Schweizer

A hardcover edition of this book was originally published in 2005
by Doubleday.

Published in the United States by Broadway Books,
an imprint of The Doubleday Broadway Publishing Group,
a division of Random House, Inc., New York.

www.broadwaybooks.com

BROADWAY BOOKS and its logo, a letter B bisected on the diagonal,
are trademarks of Random House, Inc.

Book design by Nicola Ferguson

Library of Congress Cataloging-in-Publication Data
is on file with the Library of Congress.

ISBN-13: 978-0-7679-1902-9
ISBN-10: 0-7679-1902-5

PRINTED IN THE UNITED STATES OF AMERICA

1   3   5   7   9   10   8   6   4   2

First Paperback Edition

To Ron Robinson
Who ignited my interest in politics and ideas
more than two decades ago. Thanks.

▶▶ contents

▶▶ *acknowledgments*

First I want to thank the liberals profiled here for living such inconsistent lives. Perhaps this book will get you to rethink a few things.

I owe a great deal of thanks to the people at Doubleday who have stood faithfully behind *Do As I Say*. My editor, Adam Bellow, is undoubtedly one of the best in the business. He not only helped immensely with the concept, but also the execution. Thanks again, Adam, for your commitment and friendship. Doubleday publisher Stephen Rubin and editor in chief Bill Thomas have been the consummate professionals, enthusiastically behind this project even though they probably don't agree with much of what I've written. Special thanks also to Nicole Dewey.

I received considerable help from a number of young professionals and students in compiling the material for this book. I'm particularly indebted to Cory Shreckengost, Mary Guese, Andy Lee, and Tim Lundquist, for running down those rabbit trails to find interesting facts and information.

I've now been a fellow at the Hoover Institution for seven years. The history and resources of Hoover are great, but it's the people that make it a very special place. Thanks to John Raisian for always being accessible and supportive; Tom Henriksen and Peter Robinson for your sage advice; Noel Kolak for your enthusiasm and support; and to all the donors who make our work possible.

To my friends I say thanks for your support and encouragement: Wynton Hall, Tim Watkins, Tim Ireland, Richard Alberton, Dayton Jones, Mike Short, Marc Thiessen, the Overholsers, the Steigners, the Enwrights, the Youngs, Bob Angelotti, Paul Kengor, Tom Sylte, Floyd Brown, Cap Weinberger, Newt Gingrich, Ron Robinson, Mark Perry, and Owen and Bernadette Smith.

Finally, to my family, what can I say? I love you and feel blessed every day that you love me. Rochelle, Jack, and Hannah, thanks for being with me every single day. Mom, Maria, Joe, Daniel and Adam, Evelyn, and Rich—my life is better and richer, knowing you.

The liberals I know and am related to would never forgive me if I didn't remind the readers that the author alone is responsible for the contents of this book.

Do As I Say
(NOT AS I DO)

▶▶ *Introduction*

The Do-As-I-Say Liberals

In 1998, popular conservative radio host Dr. Laura Schlessinger was deeply embarrassed when it was revealed that she had posed for some nude photos in her youth. Millions of Americans listen to Dr. Laura every week as she offers advice on marriage, family, parenting, and other issues from a traditional-values perspective. Her books, which expound on the wisdom of the Ten Commandments and traditional marriage roles, have sold millions of copies. So when nude photos of a young Dr. Laura surfaced on the Internet, her critics were quick to pounce. "How is the best-selling author of 'Ten Stupid Things Women Do to Mess Up Their Lives' going to spin *this*?" asked *Salon*.[1]

In June 2003 the *Washington Monthly* and *Newsweek* revealed that William J. Bennett, who had written a string of best-selling books promoting virtue (and excoriating the moral failings of Bill Clinton), was a heavy gambler.

Liberal columnist Michael Kinsley gleefully predicted that Bennett's hypocrisy would spell the end of his moral credibility, declaring, "As the joyous word spread, crack flowed like water through inner-city streets, family court judges began handing out free divorces, children lit bonfires of *The Book of Virtues, More Virtuous Virtues, Who Cheesed My Virtue?, Moral Tails: Virtue for Dogs,* etc. And cynics everywhere thought, for just a moment: Maybe there is a God after all."

The Soros-funded Center for American Progress announced that it would offer a "Bill Bennett Hypocrisy Award" for other conservatives who were "caught" in a similar fashion. They got their first opportunity a few months later when it was revealed that radio talk show host Rush Limbaugh was addicted to the prescription drug OxyContin, which he had been originally prescribed after back surgery in 1995. Liberals called him the ultimate hypocrite, a law-and-order man caught breaking the law. Al Franken could barely contain his joy at the humiliation of his rival and bête noire, openly expressing the hope that Limbaugh would be arrested and go to jail.

None of these bullets fired by liberals directly hit their mark, however. Dr. Laura's embarrassing photos were shot in the 1970s, well before she became a prominent traditionalist. "With the mind-set I have now, there are certain things I would not have done," she told *Vanity Fair* contritely before the photos became public. "I am repentant; I have moved on." Bennett, while extolling the importance of honesty, integrity, and virtue, had never singled out gambling as immoral, and he had made no real effort to hide his activity. Though on his trips to Vegas he largely confined his gambling to his room, it was well known in Washington that he enjoyed a good game of high-stakes poker. Nor has anyone bothered to investigate the real scandal here, namely how this private information about a casino guest was leaked to the press—especially in a town whose promotional slogan is, "What happens here, stays here." The lack of curiosity about this on the part of mainstream media is telling.

Rush Limbaugh had indeed gone after drug addicts and was a happy warrior in the antidrug campaign earlier in his career. But once his illegal use of OxyContin began in 1996, he didn't return to the subject. When the *National Enquirer* published a list of Limbaugh quotes about drug abuse, all but one dated from 1993. The Center for American Progress could add only one more—a comment Limbaugh made about Jerry Garcia being "another dead drug addict." But even that was from August 1995. Amazingly, no one could find an incriminating quote, even though Limbaugh had been on the air for more than six thousand hours from the time he started his addiction to the time it was exposed.

Limbaugh faced prosecution on drug charges by a legal team that could only be described as highly motivated. Despite its reputation for going after dealers and not users, the West Palm Beach Prosecutor's Office tried to obtain Limbaugh's medical records without his knowledge (thereby skirting subpoena rules). They released confidential correspondence between the prosecutor and Limbaugh's lawyer. Portions of his medical records ended up on cable television. Betty Castor, the Democratic nominee for the U.S. Senate in Florida, explained that her son, who worked in the prosecutor's office, would "fight very hard to put Rush Limbaugh away . . . or at least get him off the air."[2]

Hypocrisy has proved to be a wonderful weapon for liberals in their war against conservatives. When a religious mountebank like Jimmy Swaggart or a pro-family politician gets caught cheating on his wife, their political enemies use the charge to good effect. When the president of conservative Hillsdale College was forced to resign after a scandal involving the suicide of his daughter-in-law, with whom (to make matters worse) it was discovered he was having an affair, liberal newspaper columns resounded with cries of "I told you so." Newt Gingrich was roundly excoriated for allegedly divorcing his first wife as she lay in a hospital bed, after setting himself up as a champion of "family values." Meanwhile, liberal spokesmen do their level best to milk these misfortunes for all they are worth. When *New York Times* columnist Maureen Dowd gets on the subject, this secular liberal suddenly gets religious and starts talking about heaven and hell. "Okay," she told Chris Matthews on *The Chris Matthews Show*, "I'll predict that the rapture's coming and you and I, Chris, are going up, and all these hypocritical conservatives who tell people not to do stuff but then they get caught doing are not."[3]

Howard Dean, chairman of the Democratic National Committee, did an impression of Rush Limbaugh at a gathering for Democrats and included the sound of someone snorting cocaine. In a May 2005 appearance on *Meet the Press,* he defended his parody on the grounds that "hypocrisy is a value that I think has been embraced by the Republican Party. We get lectured by people all day long about moral values by people who have got their own moral shortcomings." Dean promised, "I will use whatever position I have in order to root out hypocrisy."[4]

Unlike most liberals, however, conservatives understand and accept the reality of hypocrisy as part of the human condition. The notion of original sin, or flawed human nature, is embraced by pretty much every conservative philosophy. Indeed, it is enshrined in our very system of government. Conservatives believe in cautious change and a limited government of checks and balances precisely because as human beings we are flawed and prone to sin and vice. As James Madison argued in the Federalist Papers, people can't turn into angels, no matter what policies you adopt.

Conservatives do tend to set themselves up as defenders of public morality and virtue . . . only to stumble and fall. But in most instances, when conservatives betray their publicly stated principles, they harm only themselves and their families. Moreover, just because some people don't live up to these high principles doesn't invalidate them or make them wrong. Conservative principles are like guardrails on a winding road: They can be constraining and even annoying, but smash through them at your own risk.

Yet for all the talk about conservative hypocrisy and the endless chatter about Limbaugh, Bennett, Dr. Laura, Newt Gingrich, and others, there has been very little investigation into the prevalence of hypocrisy on the left. Liberal talk show host Alan Colmes has gone so far as to say that hypocrisy is essentially a conservative disease, something liberals can't catch. "It's much more difficult for a liberal to be hypocritical than it is for a conservative," Colmes observed in his book *Red, White & Liberal*. "Conservatives are more likely to take absolutist positions because they see the world in stark, good versus evil terms. Because the world isn't just black and white, conservatives back themselves into ideological corners from which they cannot be easily extracted."[5]

Colmes must be living in a parallel universe—watching a different television and reading different magazines and books. He is certainly correct that conservatives can and do take "absolutist positions," especially on questions of morality. But liberals do the same when it comes to social and economic questions. They speak with haughty moral certitude about matters of economic justice, inequality, and fairness. They strike a pose of fighting for the little guy against the rich and powerful. They consider themselves in the vanguard of the battle against racism and oppression, and paint themselves as defenders of the environment against rapacious industrial capitalism. Confident of the purity of their motives, they are likewise sublimely convinced of their opponents' evil intentions. Unlike conservatives, who they see as motivated by base drives and greedy passions, liberals pride themselves on being committed and selfless. In short, liberals pose as our moral superiors, more altruistic, more sensitive to the needs of the oppressed, and less concerned with money and self-interest than anyone else.

There is another important difference between conservatives and liberals. Conservatives often (but certainly not always) confine their moral beliefs to the realm of personal conduct and responsibility. Liberals on the other hand seek to legislate their beliefs and impose them on others. To correct what they see as economic and social injustice, they support a whole litany of policies and principles: progressive taxes, affirmative action, greater corporate regulation, a steep inheritance tax, strict environmental curbs, children's rights, labor unions, consumer rights, and much more. Moreover, these policies are not advanced on pragmatic grounds alone, but because they are "right" and "just." Raising taxes is not just a question of balancing the budget, but of correcting a social wrong. It's not enough to encourage the rich to give to the poor, they must be compelled to do so through taxation because it is "unfair" for some to have "too much" while others live in poverty.

In the sixties, the New Left coined the phrase "the personal is political." What they meant was that they saw no distinction between public and private spheres of morality and conduct. No area was off limits to political activism. Family life, private conduct, and personal morality were all fair game for political activism.

But I wondered—is the political also personal? Do the prophets of the liberal/left apply the political ideas they espouse to their personal lives? Beyond preaching affirmative action and racial diversity, do they, given the chance, actually practice these ideals in their own lives? When they proclaim the necessity of "soaking the rich" in the name of social justice, do they allow their own assets to be drenched? When they preach conservation, fuel efficiency, and respect for the environment, do they apply those principles to their own lives and private property?

When they champion the cause of organized labor, do they hire union workers themselves? When they attack capitalism as evil and unjust, do they eschew private property and practice socialism? I decided to find out for myself.

Watching television one night, I saw Terry McAuliffe, then chairman of the Democratic National Committee, expounding on the importance of labor unions as an essential check on corporate power and to guarantee a living wage for American workers. Living in Florida, I knew that McAuliffe had been in the homebuilding business around Orlando. Did he use union labor when he was chairman of Orlando-based American Heritage Homes? A quick call to the Carpenter's and Lather's Local No. 1765 revealed that McAuliffe was using "cheap immigrant labor" instead of union employees, paying them six to seven dollars an hour. The Florida Building and Construction Trades Council confirmed that under McAuliffe, there was "little or no union relationship" with American Heritage Homes. (This is a double slap to organized labor: In addition to championing unions, McAuliffe has made millions over the years through business dealings with union pension funds—unions whose members he himself would not hire.)

A few days later, someone sent me a copy of a speech delivered by the feminist writer bell hooks (the nom de plume of Gloria Watkins). One of the nation's leading feminists, she has given thousands of lectures on campuses around the country and her books are assigned in dozens of courses. In her speech, as in her books, she roundly attacked and demonized men, capitalism, and "patriarchy." In one of her most famous essays, she fantasizes about killing an anonymous man on the bus, considering it an opportunity to strike a blow against patriarchy. Living a life gripped by a principled hatred of male domination seemed like a pretty difficult existence. But then I ran across a warm profile of Ms. hooks in the *Chronicle of Higher Education,* which explained that her radical pose is merely a "persona." "While bell hooks writes about 'sexism and misogyny,' " the paper reported, the militant feminist was disappointed because she "longs for flowers from a man" instead of the self-bought lilies sitting on her dining room table. In other words, she tells young women to do without men and reject patriarchy while privately pining away for romance. When asked about this contradiction, hooks admitted that she didn't really practice what she preached. "I haven't really tried to take on the identity of bell hooks," she explained. "It's been very much a writing name, and now more of a writing persona."[6] I guess that makes it okay then.

In 2003 the Supreme Court deliberated on an affirmative action case involving the University of Michigan. When the decision came down in favor of that policy, it was greeted as a victory by Democrats. I wondered: Do Democrats in Congress practice affirmative action themselves? I soon found out that they were exempt from federal affirmative action requirements. But then I discovered something even more intriguing. According to the *National Journal,* a survey of congressional staffers revealed that Democrats hired black employees at the same rate as Republicans—2 percent.[7] These advocates of affirmative action were having it both ways: While attacking their opponents as racists, they failed to implement a higher standard themselves. What's more, no one in the press seemed to care about this glaring hypocrisy.

One night I caught Katrina vanden Heuvel on *Hardball* talking about taxes with Chris Matthews. The fiery editor of *The Nation* was striking a typical class warrior pose, upset because the rich were not paying their fair share in taxes. It's a theme she sounds regularly, fulminating about tax cuts "whose main purpose is to add to the abundance of the super-rich." She wants to "afflict the comfortable," she says, trotting out the old leftist cliché. The inheritance tax? By all means keep it so that economic justice may be done.

But when I checked into her background, I discovered that this trust-fund heiress (the best-dressed leftist on television) might better be thought of as Katrina the Princess Warrior. The Princeton-educated granddaughter of Jules Stein, founder of the mega–entertainment conglomerate MCA, vanden Heuvel has inherited millions of dollars through a series of trusts that her grandfather established with the help of legendary tax attorney John Wright. When Stein died, a big chunk of his investments were safely sheltered in trust funds. But the IRS determined that one investment device, Project Notes, containing $9 million, was not exempt. The family sued the IRS to avoid paying more than $2 million in estate taxes. Vanden Heuvel was an editor at *The Nation* at the time, and the estate fought the case all the way to the Supreme Court, which ruled against the family.[8] Does this glaring hypocrisy give vanden Heuvel a moment's pause? Apparently not.

I subsequently ran across an article about Princeton professor Peter Singer, the nation's leading proponent of utilitarianism, expounding on the need for our society to embrace infanticide and euthanasia for the severely handicapped or disabled. "The notion that human life is sacred just because it's human life is medieval," he continued, talking about the treatment of the hopelessly ill. In Singer's world, people with a whole host of ailments, including Alzheimer's, cease to be persons because they cannot reason, remember, or recognize others. Thus they should have their lives ended prematurely.[9] Singer has earned praise from the left for this Nietzschean hardness.[10] Then I learned that Singer's own mother has Alzheimer's. Moreover, far from embracing his own moral ethic, Singer hired a group of health care workers to look after her. A good son, I thought—no doubt his mother is thankful that she raised such an accomplished hypocrite.[11]

During the 2004 campaign, when Sen. John Kerry explained that the "super-rich" were not paying their fair share, he presented it as a question not just of revenue but of personal morality. I wondered: Were John Kerry and his wife, Teresa Heinz Kerry, fulfilling their social and moral responsibility? The Kerrys have a net worth exceeding $700 million, placing them among the very richest Americans. Yet when I checked their tax returns, I discovered that they were paying only 15 percent of their income in taxes. According to the IRS, the average American making $200,000 already pays 25 percent. Kerry, who pays 10 percent less, thought that percentage should be higher.

Were these isolated cases? Were these instances of liberal hypocrisy just random quirks, or part of a broader phenomenon? Answering these questions is more than an exercise in gotcha journalism. It is of central importance in evaluating the validity and usefulness of liberal ideas.

I therefore decided to examine in depth the ideas and actions of a number of prominent liberals. I tried to weed out clear charlatans and focused on liberal leaders and spokesmen who are generally esteemed by their constituents and have an influence on the broader culture, either through the sales of their books, appearances in the media, financial contributions to the liberal cause, or actual political power. In the end I settled on eleven individuals—a mix of activists, politicians, commentators and authors, cultural icons, business leaders, and academics. Each in their own way has enormous influence within the liberal/left and all are important voices in the American public debate.

Using IRS records, court depositions, news reports, financial disclosures, and their own statements, I sought to answer a particular question: Do these liberal leaders and activists actually practice what they preach?

What I found was a stunning record of open and shameless hypocrisy. Those who champion the cause of organized labor had developed various methods to avoid paying union wages or shunned unions altogether. Those who believe that the rich need to pay more in taxes proved especially adept at avoiding taxes themselves. Critics of capitalism and corporate enterprise frequently invested in the very companies they denounced. Those who espouse strict environmental regulations worked vigorously to sidestep them when it came to their own businesses and properties. Those who advocate steep inheritance taxes to promote fairer income distribution hid their investments in trusts or exotic overseas locales to reduce their own tax liability. Those who are strong proponents of affirmative action rarely practiced it themselves, and some had abysmal records when it came to hiring minorities. Those who proclaim themselves champions of civil liberties when it comes to criminal or terrorist cases went to extraordinary lengths to curtail the civil liberties of others when they felt threatened or just inconvenienced. Advocates of gun control had no problem making sure that an arsenal of weapons was available to protect them from dangerous criminals. And when it came to family matters, I found similar inconsistencies. Several prominent liberals who ridiculed abstinence-based sex education programs purposely enrolled their children in schools that featured such programs. Advocates of expanded rights for children and opponents of media censorship were actually strict parents. And feminists who attacked "romance" and "patriarchy" were quietly attracted to these themselves.

Nor were these contradictions between what liberals said and what they did the result of some hasty decision or oversight. Rather, they were well-established patterns of behavior. They were signs of a deeply consistent inconsistency, of hypocrisies repeated over the course of years, sometimes decades, requiring deliberate planning and action. It seemed impossible for the individuals in question not to be aware of them.

When Bill Bennett, Rush Limbaugh, and Dr. Laura suffered personal exposure and embarrassment, they took public responsibility for their actions, acknowledging their failures and shortcomings. It is hard to find an instance where a prominent liberal or leftist has done the same. Those whom I contacted personally had no interest in doing so.

Part of the reason is simple: They don't want to give ammunition to their political enemies. But there is also a more compelling reason. Limbaugh, Bennett, and Dr. Laura were the first to admit that by contradicting their own principles they had *damaged* their lives and reputations. They were not better off for having done what they did. But for liberals, the case is quite the opposite. When liberals abandon their principles and engage in hypocrisy, they often *improve* their lives. What does that tell us about which ideas are superior?

Much of what follows will strike many people as a revelation precisely because liberal hypocrisy gets a big fat pass from the liberal press, which fails to subject prominent liberals to the kind of intense personal scrutiny that is commonly meted out to conservatives.

What follows are the fruits of my (by no means exhaustive) investigation into the affairs of some leading liberal spokesmen. Readers will note, however, that I have confined myself largely to their financial and business arrangements rather than focusing on their private lives and personal morality. Such degraded (and degrading) attacks on people's gambling or addictions or obesity or sexual proclivities I leave to my colleagues on the liberal/left. There is anger, even hatred, in these liberal attacks against conservatives, a palpable desire to humiliate their opponents and expose them to personal ridicule. But that is not my motive or my purpose. I am not interested in liberals' personal moral failings—failings to which all of us are prone—but in the quality of their ideas, and specifically in whether they actually live by the ideas and commitments they so confidently prescribe to the rest of us.

For despite the fact that they often speak of them with genuine conviction, these do-as-I-say liberals don't actually trust their ideas enough to apply them at home. Instead, when it comes to the things that matter most in their personal lives, they tend to behave—ironically—more like conservatives than liberals. Which can only make one wonder: If their liberal prescriptions don't really work for them as individuals, how can they work for the rest of us?

NOAM CHOMSKY

Social Parasite, Economic Protectionist, Amoral Defense Contractor

I never thought a self-described socialist dissident and anti-imperialist crusader could be so thin-skinned.

I had sent Noam Chomsky several e-mails, questioning him in a mild but insistent way about his personal wealth, investments, and legal maneuvers to avoid paying taxes. What I got back was a stream of invective and some of the most creative logic I have ever seen in my life. No wonder he is considered one of the most important linguists in the world; he's adept at twisting words.

Noam Chomsky doesn't look like your typical revolutionary. The soft-spoken MIT professor is thin and poorly dressed, with a shy smile and gentle manner. But when he speaks or writes about America, the Pentagon, and capitalism, this self-appointed "champion of the ordinary guy" erupts as if the wrath of God had descended from heaven.

Chomsky doesn't think America is a free country: "The American electoral system is a series of four-year dictatorships." There is no real free press, only "brainwashing under freedom." In his book *What Uncle Sam Really Wants*, he describes an America on par with Nazi Germany. "Legally speaking," he says, "there's a very solid case for impeaching every American president since the Second World War. They've all been either outright war criminals or involved in serious war crimes." His views on capitalism? Put it up there with Nazism. Don't even ask about the Pentagon. It's the most vile institution on the face of the earth.

Chomsky may sound like a crank, but he's a crank taken seriously around the world. Hundreds of thousands of college students read his books. Michael Moore has claimed him as a mentor of sorts, and the leadership of the AFL-CIO has gone to him for political advice. *The Guardian* declares that he "ranks with Marx, Shakespeare, and the Bible as one of the most quoted sources in the humanities." Robert Barsky, in a glowing biography, claims that Chomsky "will be for future generations what Galileo, Descartes, Newton, Mozart or Picasso have been for ours."[1]

Though he originally made his name as a professor of linguistics, his political radicalism has made him a superstar. He is embraced by entertainers and actors as some kind of modern-day Buddha. Bono, of the band U2, calls him "the Elvis of Academia." On *Saturday Night Live*, a cast member carried a copy of his collected works during one skit in obvious homage to him. In the film *Good Will Hunting*, Matt Damon played a brilliant young man who quotes Chomsky like some Old Testament prophet. The rock band Pearl Jam even featured Chomsky at some of their concerts. With thousands packed into a concert hall, the slender Chomsky would come out onstage and ruminate on the horrors of American capitalism. Other rock bands have proclaimed him their hero, and one even named itself "Chomsky" in veneration.

Chomsky regularly lectures before thousands of people. In Blue State strongholds like Berkeley, California, and Cambridge, Massachusetts, hundreds are turned away at the door. Even in Texas, the heart of Bush Country, a recent campus appearance brought two thousand to the auditorium. David Barsamian, host of *Alternative Radio,* explains that the professor "is for many of us our rabbi, our preacher, our rinpoche, our pundit, our imam, our sensei."[2]

Chomsky plays the part. He dresses simply, proclaims his lack of interest in material things, and holds forth like a modern-day Gandhi. His low-key, deliberate manner is part of his secret. MIT colleague Steven Pinker recalls, "My first impression of him was, like many people, one of awe."[3]

Despite his voluminous output, Chomsky's message is remarkably simple: Do you see horror and evil in the world? Capitalism and the American military-industrial complex are to blame. He has charged that the crimes of democratic capitalism are "monstrously worse" than those of communism.[4] *Spin* magazine has called him "a capitalist's worst nightmare." He considers the United States a "police state."

Chomsky often calls himself an "American dissident,"

comparing himself to dissidents in the former Soviet Union. He calls his critics "commissars" and says their tactics are familiar to any student of police state behavior. When asked by a reporter why he is ignored by official Washington, he said, "It's been done throughout history. How were dissidents treated in the Soviet Union?"[5] (Hint: They weren't "ignored"; they were harassed or imprisoned by the KGB.) Yet despite its manifest absurdity, visions of Chomsky as some sort of American Sakharov have caught on. In Great Britain he has been welcomed by Labor MPs and called America's "dissident-in-chief."

But Chomsky's image and persona, carefully cultivated and encouraged by his followers over the decades, is nothing more than a well-constructed charade. Chomsky has built a highly successful career by abandoning the very ideas and principles he claims to hold dear. Indeed, his greatest accomplishment is not intellectual but entrepreneurial: He has figured out how to make a nice living as a self described "anarchist-socialist" dissident in a capitalist society. Disdaining the petty contradictions that limit other men's achievements, he has marketed himself as a courageous truth-teller constantly threatened with censorship while publishing dozens of books and holding a tenured position at one of the world's most prestigious universities. Most audaciously, he has enriched himself by taking millions from the Pentagon while denouncing it as the epitome of evil.

This hypocrisy is particularly stunning because he first entered the national political stage in 1967 with an impassioned article in the *New York Review of Books* called "The Responsibility of Intellectuals," in which he challenged the nation's writers and thinkers "to speak the truth and to expose lies." He attacked establishment figures like Arthur Schlesinger Jr. and Henry Kissinger, claiming that they demonstrated a "hypocritical moralism" by professing to be something they were not. Chomsky long ago embraced the leftist notion that the personal is political, and that intellectuals should be held strictly accountable for what they say and do. His advice to young people in a recent interview: "Think for yourselves, and observe elementary moral principles, such as taking responsibility for your actions, or inactions."[6]

Chomsky has made a career out of scrutinizing and passing judgment on others. But he has always worked to avoid similar scrutiny. As he told a National Public Radio (NPR) interviewer, he was not going to discuss "the house, the children, personal life—anything like that . . . This is not about a person. It's about ideas and principles." But in a very real way it is all about Chomsky. Is this self-professed American Sakharov really who he claims to be? Does he live by the "moral truisms" with which he has pummeled others over the past four decades?

Let's start with Chomsky's bête noire, the American military.

To hear Chomsky describe it, the Pentagon has got to be one of the most evil institutions in world history. He has called it several times "the most hideous institution on this earth" and declares that it "constitutes a menace to human life."[7] More to the point, the military has no business being on college campuses, whether recruiting, providing money for research, or helping students pay for college. Professors shouldn't work with the Pentagon, he has said, and instead should fight racism, poverty, and repression.[8] Universities shouldn't take Pentagon research money because it ends up serving the Pentagon's sinister goal of "militarizing" American society.[9] He's also against college students getting ROTC scholarships, and from Vietnam to the Gulf War he has helped in efforts to drive the program off college campuses.[10]

So imagine my surprise when I discovered Chomsky's lucrative secret: He himself has been paid millions by the Pentagon over the last forty years. Conveniently, he also claims that it is morally acceptable.

Chomsky's entrance into the world of academe came in 1955 when he received his PhD. He was already a political radical, having determined at the age of ten that capitalism and the American military-industrial complex were dangerous and repugnant. You might think that Chomsky, being a linguist, worked for the MIT Linguistics Department when he joined the faculty. But in fact, Chomsky chose to work for the Research Laboratory of Electronics, which was funded entirely by the Pentagon and a few multinational corporations. Because of the largesse from this "menace to human life," lab employees like Chomsky enjoyed a light teaching load, an extensive staff, and a salary that was roughly 30 percent higher than equivalent positions at other universities.

Over the next half century, Chomsky would make millions by cashing checks from "the most hideous institution on this earth."

He wrote his first book, *Syntactic Structures,* with grants from the U.S. Army (Signal Corps), the air force (Office of Scientific Research, Air Research, and Development Command), and the Office of Naval Research. Though Chomsky says that American corporations "are just as totalitarian as Bolshevism and fascism," he apparently didn't mind taking money from them, either, because the Eastman Kodak Corporation also provided financial support.

His next book, *Aspects of the Theory of Syntax,* was produced with money from the Joint Services Electronic Program (U.S. Army, U.S. Navy, and U.S. Air Force) as well as the U.S. Air Force Electronic Systems Division.

Serving this "fascist institution" (as he has repeatedly called it) became a family affair when his wife, Carol, also an accomplished linguist, signed on for Pentagon work participating in a DoD-funded project called "Baseball."[11]

Why would the Pentagon fund research into linguistics? Were they simply interested in advancing science? Chomsky would call anyone who believed such a thing supremely naïve. As Chomsky well knew, his work in linguistics was considered vital by the air force and others to improve their "increasingly large investment in so-called 'command and control' computer systems" that were being used "to support our forces in Vietnam." As air force colonel Edmund P. Gaines put it in 1971, "Since the computer cannot 'understand' English, the commanders' queries must be translated into a language that the computer can deal with; such languages resemble English very little, either in their form or in the ease with which they are learned and used."[12]

Given Chomsky's high profile and shrill rhetoric, it is amazing that he has never been called on this glaring hypocrisy. The one example I could find when it actually became an issue was back in 1967, when Chomsky famously challenged his fellow professors to take moral responsibility for their actions, denounce the Pentagon, and admit that they were compromised by advising the government. George Steiner, a professor at Columbia, wrote Chomsky a letter that was published in the *New York Review of Books,* asking him earnestly: What action do you urge? And he directly asked: "Will Noam Chomsky announce that he will stop teaching at MIT or anywhere in this country so long as torture and napalm go on?" Chomsky had urged people to avoid paying taxes, resist the draft, and protest the war. He even advocated civil violence as a possible solution. But Chomsky balked at Steiner's suggestion. He could have publicly resigned, denounced the Pentagon, and taken a faculty position at any leading university in the country. But Chomsky wasn't willing to give up his position. Since then, he has tried to avoid discussing the subject. Along the way, he has been paid a nice salary for more than four decades courtesy of the Pentagon.

Armed with evidence of Chomsky's willingness to accept millions in salary and benefits from the Pentagon while trying to run ROTC off campus, I wrote him an e-mail asking him to explain himself. To his credit, Chomsky did respond. But what he sent back was less than convincing.

"I think we should be responsible for what we do, not for the bureaucratic question of who stamps the paycheck," he wrote, adding provocatively, "Do you think you are not working for the Pentagon? Ask yourself about the origins of the computer and the Internet you are now using."

Somehow, the fact that I use the Internet, which was created by the U.S. military, not only means that I am "working for the Pentagon," it is the moral equivalent of Chomsky himself growing wealthy on Pentagon contracts. I don't know about you, but I'm still waiting for my check.

Intriguingly, Chomsky seems to have taken me for someone even farther to the left than he is. Thus as our correspondence continued, he suddenly grew defensive and accused me of attacking "those who have not been living up to your exalted standards."

But of course it was Chomsky himself who had created this "exalted" standard by condemning those who might consider taking grants or scholarships from the Pentagon.

When Chomsky appears on college campuses, he usually dresses in a rumpled shirt and jacket. He is identified with dozens of left-wing causes and professes to speak for the poor, the oppressed, and the "victims of capitalism." But Chomsky is himself a shrewd capitalist, worth millions, with money in the dreaded and evil stock market, and at least one tax haven to cut down on those pesky inheritance taxes that he says are so important.

Chomsky describes himself as a "socialist" whose goal is a "post-capitalist society worth living in or fighting for."[13] He has called capitalism a "grotesque catastrophe" and a doctrine "crafted to induce hopelessness, resignation, and despair." When speaking about class struggle, Chomsky uses terms like "us" versus "them." *Them* includes "the top ten percent of taxpayers" (the bracket he himself occupies). *Us,* he says with truly audacious dishonesty, includes the other 90 percent. He further polishes his radical credentials by boasting about how he loves to spend time with "unemployed working class, activists of one kind or another, those considered to be riff-raff."[14]

Yet this man of the people, who is among the top 2 percent in the United States in net wealth, moved his family out of Cambridge, Massachusetts—hardly a working-class district to begin with—to the even more affluent wooded suburb of Lexington, where he was even less likely to mingle with blue-collar types. Moreover, he made the move around the time forced busing was being imposed on the Boston area; Lexington was exempt from the court order. Today, America's leading socialist owns a home worth over $850,000 and a vacation home in Wellfleet, Massachusetts, valued in excess of $1.2 million. Chomsky's home on the Cape is smack in the middle of a state park, which prevents any condos from going up nearby and obstructing his view. And don't look for oppressed minorities in either neighborhood. This self-described admirer of the Black Panthers, who says intellectuals must combat "all forms of racism" and complains that America "excludes" blacks from large parts of the country, owns a home in a town with a black population of 1.1 percent.[15]

Chomsky is not lonely in Wellfleet. His close friend and fellow radical Howard Zinn, author of *A People's History of America,* also makes his home there. Zinn has made a comfortable living over the years trumpeting his economic idea "that there should be no disproportions in the world," that everyone should basically have the same amount of wealth. He is also quick to pull the trigger and use words like *perpetual racism* and *racist segregation* in American society.[16] For all of his talk, Zinn owns two homes in expensive lily-white Wellfleet and a third in multicultural Auburndale (minority population 3.3 percent). A bit disproportionate, don't you think?

Chomsky's considerable fortune has translated not only into desirable real estate holdings but also a nice sailboat. Money is never a problem. As a former student explained to the radical magazine *Mother Jones:* "When his last car broke down, he simply walked into the nearest car dealership he could find and said, 'I'd like a big car. Any big car will do.' " (Chomsky denies it happened.)[17]

Another persistent theme in Chomsky's work has been class warfare. He has frequently lashed out against the "massive use of tax havens to shift the burden to the general population and away from the rich" and criticized the concentration of wealth in "trusts" by the wealthiest 1 percent.[18] The American tax code is rigged with "complicated devices for ensuring that the poor—like eighty percent of the population—pay off the rich."[19] Nor does he have any patience for tax cuts. "A tax rebate is exactly equivalent to a welfare payment," he says.[20]

But trusts can't be all bad. After all, Chomsky, with a net worth north of $2 million, decided to create one for himself. A few years back he went to Boston's venerable white-shoe law firm Palmer and Dodge and, with the help of a tax attorney specializing in "income-tax planning," set up an irrevocable trust to protect his assets from Uncle Sam. He named his tax attorney (every socialist radical needs one!) and a daughter as trustees. To the Diane

Chomsky Irrevocable Trust (named for another daughter) he has assigned the copyright of several of his books, including multiple international editions.[21] Chomsky favors the estate tax and massive income redistribution—just not the redistribution of *his* income. No reason to let radical politics get in the way of sound estate planning.

When I challenged Chomsky about his trust in our e-mail exchange, this radical socialist suddenly started to sound very bourgeois: "I don't apologize for putting aside money for my children and grandchildren." He offered no explanation for why he condemns others who are equally proud of their provision for their children and who try to protect their assets from Uncle Sam. Although he did say that the tax shelter is okay because he and his family are "trying to help suffering people."

Indeed, Chomsky is rich precisely because he has been such an enormously successful capitalist. Despite the antiprofit rhetoric, like any other corporate capitalist, he has turned himself into a brand name. As John Lloyd puts it, writing critically in the lefty *New Statesman,* Chomsky is among those "open to being 'commodified'—that is, to being simply one of the many wares of a capitalist media marketplace, in a way that the badly paid and overworked writers and journalists for the revolutionary parties could rarely be."[22]

Chomsky's business works something like this. He gives speeches on college campuses around the country at $12,000 a pop, often dozens of times a year. Can't go and hear him in person? No problem: You can go online and download clips from earlier speeches—for a fee. You can hear Chomsky talk for one minute about "Property Rights"; it will cost you seventy-nine cents. You can also buy a CD with clips from previous speeches for $12.99.

But books are Chomsky's mainstay, and on the international market he has become a publishing phenomenon. The Chomsky brand means instant sales. As publicist Dana O'Hare of Pluto Press explains: "All we have to do is put Chomsky's name on a book and it sells out immediately!"

Putting his name on a book should not be confused with writing a book, because his most recent volumes are mainly transcriptions of speeches or interviews that he has conducted over the years, put between covers and sold to the general public. You might call it multilevel marketing for radicals. Chomsky has admitted as much: "If you look at the things I write—articles for Z magazine, or books for South End Press, or whatever—they are mostly based on talks and meetings and that kind of thing. But I'm kind of a parasite. I mean, I'm living off the activism of others. I'm happy to do it."[23]

Chomsky's marketing efforts shortly after September 11 give new meaning to the term "war profiteer." In the days after the tragedy, he raised his speaking fee from $9,000 to $12,000 because he was suddenly in greater demand. He also cashed in by producing another instant book. Seven Stories Press, a small publisher, pulled together interviews conducted via e-mail that Chomsky gave in the three weeks following the attack on the Twin Towers and rushed the book to press. His controversial views were hot, particularly overseas. By early December 2001, they had sold the foreign rights in nineteen different languages.[24] The book made the best-seller list in the United States, Canada, Germany, India, Italy, Japan, and New Zealand. It is safe to assume that he netted hundreds of thousands of dollars from this book alone.

Over the years, Chomsky has been particularly critical of private property rights, which he considers simply a tool of the rich, of no benefit to ordinary people (contrary to the views of such American statesmen as Jefferson, Hamilton, and Adams, for whom small-scale private ownership was the keystone of national liberty). "When property rights are granted to power and privilege, it can be expected to be harmful to most people," Chomsky wrote on a discussion board for the *Washington Post*. Intellectual property rights are equally despicable. According to Chomsky, for example, drug companies that have spent hundreds of millions of dollars developing drugs shouldn't have ownership rights to patents. Intellectual property rights "have to do with protectionism," he argues. "That's protectionism."[25]

Protectionism is a bad thing—especially when it relates to other people. But when it comes to his own published work, this advocate of open intellectual property suddenly becomes very selfish. It would not be advisable to download the audio from one of his speeches without paying the fee, warns his record company, Alternative Tentacles. (Did Andrei Sakharov have a licensing agreement with a record company?) And when it comes to his articles, you'd better keep your hands off. Go to the official Noam Chomsky web site (chomsky.info) and the warning is clear: "Material on this site is copyrighted by Noam Chomsky and/or Noam Chomsky and his collaborators.

No material on this site may be reprinted or posted on other web sites without written permission." However, the web site does give you the opportunity to "sublicense" the material if you are interested.[26]

Radicals used to think of their ideas as weapons; Chomsky sees them as a licensing opportunity.

Chomsky has even gone the extra mile to protect the copyright to some of his material by transferring ownership to his children. Profits from those works will thus be taxed at his children's lower rate. This also extends the length of time that the family is able to hold onto the copyright and protect his intellectual assets.[27]

In October 2002, radicals gathered in Philadelphia for a benefit entitled Noam Chomsky: Media and Democracy, sponsored by the Greater Philadelphia Democratic Left. For a fee of $15 you could attend the speech and hear the great man ruminate on the evils of capitalism. For another $35, you could attend a post-talk reception and he would speak directly with you. During the speech, Chomsky told the assembled crowd, "A democracy requires a free, independent, and inquiring media." After the speech, Deborah Bolling, a writer for the lefty *Philadelphia City Paper,* tried to get an interview with Chomsky. She was turned away. To talk to Chomsky, she was told, this "free, independent, and inquiring" reporter would need to pay $35 to get into the private reception.[28]

Corporate America is one of Chomsky's demons. It's hard to find anything positive he might say about American business. He paints an ominous vision of America suffering under the "unaccountable and deadly rule of corporations." He has called corporations "private tyrannies" and declared that they are "just as totalitarian as Bolshevism and fascism." Capitalism, in his words, is a "grotesque catastrophe."

But a funny thing happened on the way to the retirement portfolio. Chomsky, for all of his moral dudgeon against American corporations, finds that they make a pretty good investment. When he made investment decisions for his retirement plan at MIT, he chose not to go with a money market fund, or even a government bond fund. Instead, he threw the money into blue chips and invested in the TIAA-CREF stock fund. A look at this stock fund portfolio quickly reveals that it invests in all sorts of businesses that Chomsky says he finds abhorrent—oil companies, military contractors, pharmaceuticals, you name it.[29]

When I asked Chomsky about his investment portfolio, he reverted to a "What else can I do?" defense: "Should I live in a cabin in Montana?" he asked. It was a clever rhetorical dodge. Chomsky was declaring that there is simply no way to avoid getting involved in the stock market short of complete withdrawal from the capitalist system. He certainly knows better. In addition to money market funds and bonds, there are many alternative funds these days that allow you to invest your money in "green" or "socially responsible" enterprises. They just don't yield the maximum available return.

Chomsky has a particular tic about the oppression of women and minorities. America is a racist and sexist society, he declares. Disparities in income and the lack of women in some professions is evidence enough of systematic racism and sex discrimination. Indeed, women live in a condition of "slave labor," because they are forced to stay at home without adequate pay. The relationship between "men and women" is an example of "illegitimate authority."[30] For women there is not only a "glass ceiling" but a core "system of oppression."[31]

Chomsky has had plenty of opportunities to deal with this issue in his own life. After all, he created the linguistics and philosophy departments at MIT. For half a century he has personally hired or approved the staff and faculty. How did this champion of women and minorities do?

When you look at Chomsky's tenure in both the linguistics department and in the early years of the philosophy department, you find that his hires were almost exclusively white males. Indeed, the situation was so shockingly lopsided that in the 1980s there was "a mini-uprising" in Chomsky's linguistics department when feminist grad students pointed out that it was "all male." One former student complained to *Mother Jones*: "Chomsky thinks he is a feminist, but—at heart—he's an old-fashioned patriarch. . . . He just never really understood what the feminist movement was about." Even today, a look at the MIT Linguistics Department web site reveals that Chomsky's department is top-heavy with white males, and the support staff is made up almost entirely of women.[32]

Chomsky has also painted himself over the decades as a tireless champion of free speech and independent media. One of his most popular works in left-wing circles is

Manufacturing Consent, which argues that in capitalist societies there is really no free press. Chomsky sees the United States as being quite like a totalitarian society, only using different techniques to control the domestic population. He considers himself the ultimate champion of free speech, saying he will defend the freedom of expression of anyone, anytime, on any issue. He is a raging volcano on the subject when it comes to the Western world, with plenty of lava and ash. But when it comes to communist countries, he can barely muster a puff of smoke.

In 1970, Noam Chomsky was standing in a field in Tanh Hoa Province, North Vietnam, where he had come to support the North Vietnamese cause. After a tour, Chomsky stood up and gave a speech, describing what he had seen in the workers' paradise. "We saw luxurious fields and lovely countryside. We saw brave men and women who know how to defend their country from brutal aggression, but also to work with pride and with dignity to build a society of material prosperity, social justice, and cultural progress. I would like to express the great joy that we feel in your accomplishments." Then he began his denunciations of the United States. "In the midst of the creative achievements of the Vietnamese people, we came face to face with the savagery of a technological monster controlled by a social class, the rulers of the American empire, that has no place in the twentieth century, that has only the capacity to repress and murder and destroy." He expressed his hope that Vietnam was moving "toward the socialist society in which free, creative men control their own destiny . . . Decent people throughout the world see in your struggle a model for themselves."[33]

There is no record of Chomsky criticizing the true lack of free speech in communist Vietnam. Indeed, in his book *At War with Asia,* he described his visit there in glowing terms. Here the central paradox of Chomsky's thought emerges: He is suspicious and harshly critical of everything the United States does and discounts its official statements, and even the statements of its independent press, as propaganda; yet when it comes to Vietnam, he is sublimely credulous and believes everything he is told. Chomsky called the South Vietnamese regime in Saigon "authoritarian and repressive," but said nothing about the North Vietnamese government's massacre of three thousand civilians two years earlier in Hue, an event he already knew about.[34] This champion of free speech who claimed that corporate "lapdogs" like the *New York Times* lacked the courage to print the truth nonetheless accepted everything said to him by the director of the largest state-owned newspaper in North Vietnam (the equivalent of *Pravda*). He spent time with Premier Pham Van Dong and other high-ranking officials, again accepting everything they said, including their patently false assurances that "South Vietnam, Cambodia, and Laos will be neutral after the reunification of the country." He mentioned not one word about the status of dissidents, the lack of a free press, the fate of political prisoners, or the policy of official repression. This champion of individual freedom and dissent, this American Sakharov, went to a totalitarian country and found no dissent. Instead, he lavished praise on a brutal collectivist dictatorship.

Chomsky also praised the North Vietnamese government's plans for "land reform," which meant confiscating private lands, even from relatively poor landowners, and redistributing it to party members. In December 1967 he was equally enthused about collectivization and communization of property in Mao's China, of which he said, "one finds many things that are really quite admirable." As Chomsky wrote those words, he had just purchased his vacation home in Wellfleet. Good thing the Viet Cong weren't running Cape Cod!

In October 2003, Chomsky paid a visit to Cuba, another totalitarian dictatorship. When he arrived, he was greeted as a superstar by Vice President Ricardo Alarcon. "It is the first time that Noam Chomsky is in Cuba," he said, "but Cuba has always been in him."[35]

Chomsky was there to participate in an academic conference. Before it was over, he was speaking before an audience that included Fidel Castro. Later he spoke before smaller groups and then made an appearance on state-owned Radio Havana. Here was a unique opportunity for this champion of free speech to make a statement about the jailing of poets and librarians in Cuba. But when he finally turned to the subject of political dissidents, he spoke about those jailed . . . in the United States. Imprisoned on charges of spying, Chomsky called them "five patriotic Cuban prisoners." Nary a word about the thousands of political prisoners being held in Cuba's gulag.[36] Instead, he effusively praised Fidel Castro. "Cuba has become a symbol of courageous resistance to attack."[37]

During his visit, Chomsky also saw the publication of a Spanish-language version of one of his books, titled *La Jornada,* with a foreword by Ricardo Alarcon.

On both of these occasions, Chomsky expressed his genuine affection for these communist dictatorships. In Vietnam he made a point of saying, "I've had a remarkable and very satisfying feeling of being entirely at home." He used a somewhat similar expression when visiting Cuba. But, of course, those countries are not Chomsky's home, and he plainly has no interest in living in either place. Instead he returns to a country that he has repeatedly compared to Nazi Germany.

Barely eight weeks after the September 11 attacks, Chomsky was in the Indian subcontinent for a series of lectures. He visited several cities in India, all the time making the usual litany of attacks on the United States. Chomsky's comments were so strong that even the Indian media was forced to admit that his speech "provided ammunition to the anti-U.S. lobbies." He was popular in India in part because "it is fashionable to be a U.S.-hater and a rebel."[38]

Chomsky had spent the past few weeks declaring that Islamic terrorism was not really a threat; America's Middle East policies had provoked any terrorist action. But when it came to his own safety, Chomsky took the threat very seriously. In order to gain admission to his lecture, you had to submit a photo ID in advance, go through a security checkpoint, and be frisked at the door. (Chomsky, who for years has denounced "police tactics" in the United States, often has undercover police attend his lectures.) Chomsky then traveled to Pakistan, just as the Afghan war was starting. He explained to an audience of thousands that Americans did not want Osama bin

Laden taken alive because they knew there was no proof that he committed the September 11 attack. In another speech, before a large crowd of government ministers, Chomsky explained that "the numbers of victims of U.S. savagery are huge right up to the present moment. For the first time, almost in two centuries, the guns have been pointed in the opposite direction." The speech was so anti-American that it drew praise from Hamid Mir, editor of the well-known pro-Taliban publication *Ausaf.* "His courage is a matter of satisfaction for those whose own intellectuals, politicians and rulers have become puppets in the hands of imperialism."

Then something interesting happened. At a private reception in Pakistan, Chomsky made what must now be an embarrassing admission. After he had spent several days denouncing the United States as an imperial aggressor, a few journalists gathered with him to discuss his visit. Muralidhar Reddy, a reporter for the Indian magazine *Frontline,* asked him where he got the courage to denounce his government and attack other governments around the world. Chomsky laughed and explained that it really didn't take much courage at all. He could speak freely precisely because of the American power that he had denounced all these years. If people in other parts of the world said such things about their governments, they would "face charges of rebellion." But he could speak freely "as I have an American passport."[39]

America is, whether Chomsky will admit it or not, the guarantor of freedom for its citizens and much of the rest of the world. It is also, for him, the land of Pentagon contracts, lucrative real estate holdings, stock market wealth, and a tax-sheltered trust for his children. Yet few have ever challenged his glaring hypocrisy or even tried to point it out. Instead, he gets a free pass from the "lapdog" press of the American imperium. Being a professional dissident, it seems, means never having to say you're sorry.

MICHAEL MOORE

Corporate Criminal, Environmental Menace, and Racist Union-Buster

Noam Chomsky may have spent decades writing screeds against American imperialism from his tenured perch at MIT, but Michael Moore is more of a street-fighter: the self-professed defender of the little guy, the common man, the vanquisher of corporate America and scourge of Stupid White Men. As a result of his irrepressible antics, Moore has become a worldwide phenomenon with a global empire built on his books, films, and speeches. These activities have reaped a financial windfall somewhere in the mid–eight figures. But Moore insists, "I haven't altered my life in any significant way." Says the Oracle of Flint, "I think once you're working class, you're always working class."[1]

The secret to Moore's success is his "street cred." The unkempt uniform he wears—baggy pants, plaid shirt, scrappy beard, and of course the ubiquitous baseball cap—perpetuates his image as someone different from other members of the Left, not an affluent bourgeois bohemian but a son of the American working class. He calls himself "an average joe" and has attacked his fellow liberals for living the lives of elitists, claiming (for example) that he gives away upward of 40 percent of his income.[2]

But this is all a carefully composed, self-serving myth, beginning with his supposed blue-collar origins and background.

Much of Moore's personal myth revolves around the Rust Belt factory town of Flint, Michigan, whose decline was the subject of his first documentary film, *Roger & Me,* and which he continues to proclaim as his home. As recently as 2003, he wrote in the *Los Angeles Times* that after the Oscars, he was heading "home to Flint." But he hadn't lived in Flint in over fourteen years. What's more, his early life was far from the hard-luck situation he describes.

When asked by the *People's Weekly World* how he relates so well to the working masses, Moore explained, "I think it's just a function of growing up in Flint." On his web site he calls himself a "Flint native." Even his e-mail address carries the mantle: mmflint@aol.com. In reality, however, Moore's family home was not in urban, blue-collar, largely black Flint, but in the nearby white middle-class town of Davison. Nor was his father just a regular working stiff struggling to make ends meet under the oppressive system of corporate capitalism. Moore's father owned his home outright, had two cars, put all four of his children through private Catholic school, and sent three kids to college. He worked for General Motors from six until two and played golf every afternoon at a private club. He had four weeks of paid vacation and retired comfortably at age fifty-three.[3]

After high school, Michael kicked around a bit (he was admitted to the University of Michigan–Flint but dropped out when he couldn't find a parking spot) and eventually began publishing a small newspaper called the *Michigan Voice*. Moore tells stories about scrimping by with little money. Absent from his narrative, however, is the fact that he had a very wealthy patron who heavily subsidized the paper. John Stuart Mott, grandson of one of the founders of General Motors, was estranged from his family and shared Moore's radical politics. John Pierson, who distributed *Roger & Me,* recalls how whenever Moore traveled to New York City, Mott would put him up at his Upper East Side guest apartment.

Before the success of *Roger & Me* in 1989, Moore claims that he never made any money, and as his success has increased in recent years, these claims of early hardship have grown in inverse proportion. First he told a reporter that he never made more than $19,000 per year. Then he told the *New Yorker,* "I never made more than fifteen thousand dollars a year." When he talked to a Canadian newspaper, his poverty plunged to $12,000.[4]

But Moore was far from the hard-luck guy who claimed that he collected bottles and cans to pay for his filmmaking projects. In 1988 he received a $50,000 advance from a New York publisher for a book about General Motors. He received another $50,000 from *Mother Jones* after he was fired from his job as editor. He also got a $20,000 grant from Ralph Nader. When he moved to

Washington, D.C., in 1988 to work for Nader, he set up house in Cleveland Park, across from the National Zoo. Hardly a blue-collar neighborhood.

In 1989, he broke onto the national stage with *Roger & Me* and since then has become very wealthy. But he continues to work hard at maintaining his image as the working-class purist completely devoted to the cause of social justice and equality.

According to an article published by the British Film Institute, when Moore flew to London to visit people at the BBC or promote a film, he took the Concorde and stayed at the Ritz. But he also allegedly booked a room at a cheap hotel down the street where he could meet with journalists and pose as a "man of humble circumstances."[5]

Nor does he live in Flint today, but owns a home on Michigan's Torch Lake, considered by National Geographic one of the three most beautiful lakes in the world. Not that Moore is doing much to preserve it. In his book *Stupid White Men,* he ridiculed George W. Bush for having an environmentally friendly ranch with a geothermal heating system, water purification and recycling system, and water-cooling machine. But Moore himself, who is worth much more than Bush, has none of these eco-friendly systems. His home, built out of seventy-year-old Michigan red pine trees, sits on ten acres. Nor, apparently, did his concern for the working man extend to his builder. Blue Chip Log Homes, a small family-run builder in nearby Maple City, actually had to put a lien on Moore's house to get the millionaire to pay them. Moore's 281 feet of prime waterfront has also been a source of local controversy. Recently Moore was cited by authorities for despoiling a wetland when he tried to expand his private beach.[6]

Moore also owns a penthouse in New York City. Indeed, for more than a decade he claimed New York as his residence. But in 2003 he switched to Michigan, no doubt in part because that year he was set to reap tens of millions in profits from *Bowling for Columbine*. In New York State, he would have been taxed at 7.7 percent. In Michigan the rate is only 3.9 percent, saving him hundreds of thousands of dollars.

This modest, working-class "regular guy" is also famously demanding when it comes to personal amenities. During a 2004 award ceremony for the left-wing organization MoveOn.org, Moore's handlers insisted that he have his own supply of imported water backstage. "Poland Spring wasn't good enough," someone at the event told *New York* magazine. "They called up to make sure he would have enough Evian."[7] Does anyone remember Archie Bunker saying, "Passez l'eau"?

For his recent book tour, Moore not only demanded first-class air transportation; he insisted on avoiding commercial flights altogether. So he traveled the country on a private jet, accompanied by a fleet of private SUVs and bodyguards.[8] The guards were encouraged to be vigilant in the face of undefined threats. Moore calls conservatives "paranoid," but at book signings his security guards would order people waiting in line to "take their hands out of their pockets."[9] Moore, who claimed in *Bowling for Columbine* that Americans buy guns out of irrational fear, surrounds himself with armed guards out of his own paranoid fear of right-wing gun nuts. One of his body-guards was recently arrested in New York City for carrying an unlicensed weapon.

Moore might be excused for embracing a revisionist history of his early childhood and enjoying the high life that he claims to reject. But his hypocrisy runs so deep, and the contradictions are so glaring and visible, that they border on the pathological.

Moore proclaims himself an economic populist who can relate to ordinary people. When speaking to American audiences, he often talks about how much he loves America and the working people of this country. But despite strenuous efforts to create the impression that he mainly targets the political elites and rich, fat CEOs, he usually goes after ordinary Americans. In its review of *Roger & Me,* the *New Yorker* made it clear that Moore's intended audience was not the working class he claimed to represent but the affluent liberal snobs of the Upper West Side. ("Members of the audience can laugh at ordinary working people and still feel that they are taking a politically correct position.") The United Auto Workers Union condemned the movie. A more recent film, *The Big One,* was allegedly an attack on corporations. But the real target ended up being ordinary working stiffs. As Cindy Fuchs writes in the lefty *Philadelphia City Paper,* "The result is—repeatedly—an embarrassed employee, a simultaneously perplexed and smug Moore, and an audience who can consider itself righteously entertained and edified."[10]

Moore admits as much himself, in candid moments. When comedian Bill Maher asked him during an interview how he got ordinary Americans to say some "really incredibly stupid" things, Moore said that it was generally very easy. "Oftentimes it's just turning the camera on and not interrupting them. And of course the people from Michigan—I grew up amongst these people, so I know them quite well. I didn't think I had to venture too far, but I believe you could literally plop a camera down in any place in the United States and find the same radius of insanity within an hour of where you put the camera."[11]

But Moore's disdain for average Americans really shines through when he speaks overseas. Moore may be popular in the United States, but by far his greatest audience is in Europe, where they love laughing at Americans.

Consider the raw numbers: Michael Moore sold 630,000 hardcover copies of *Stupid White Men* in the United States. But in Germany, with only one-third the population, he sold almost double that, 1.1 million. When his book *Dude, Where's My Country* was #1 in Germany, *Stupid White Men* was #2 and *Downsize This* was #6.[12] He has likewise sold well in Great Britain and France, and pretty much everywhere else across Europe. Along the way he has drawn praise from a wide array of anti-American critics, including the French Communist Party and Joerg Haider, leader of the Austrian far-right Freedom Party. In the Middle East, the terrorist group Hezbollah even worked with Front Row Entertainment of the United Arab Emirates to promote his film *Fahrenheit 911*.[13]

Moore's books and films sell well overseas because anti-Americanism is a popular idiom. Says Andrian Kreye of Munich, Germany's *Sueddeutsche Zeitung*, "German readers feel safe regurgitating anti-Americanism so long as it's an American who says it first." Tom Clark, a professor of history at the University of Kassel in Germany, notes, "His film and books feed negative stereotypes in Germany and the traditional belief by many here that the country is uncultured, money grubbing, materialistic, superficial and that they run around with a gun in their hands."[14] Moore even changed the subtitle of *Stupid White Men* in Germany to *Stupid White Men: Settling the Score with America under Bush.*[15]

When in the United States, Moore says he loves his country and that his beef is with George W. Bush. But when he talks overseas, he panders to the crudest anti-American stereotypes. He told an audience in Britain: "You're stuck with being connected to this country of mine, which is known for bringing sadness and misery to places around the globe." In Canada he called Americans "nuts." In Germany, the high school grad criticized Americans' intelligence and then said, to the delight of his hosts, "Should such an ignorant people lead the world?" He tells another international audience: "We've got that big shit-eating grin on our face all the time because our brains aren't loaded down." Basically his message to the world is that Americans are idiots.[16]

One constant theme in Moore's books and films is that racism is rampant in America. He's quick to pull the trigger on those he thinks are not sufficiently "inclusive." In *Bowling for Columbine,* he complains that Americans buy guns because of an irrational fear of black people. More precisely, American conservatives hate integration, mixed relationships, and minorities in general. They also refuse to discuss racism and discrimination, which is why he, as America's racial conscience, must contrive an endless series of attention-getting theatrical stunts to dramatize the issue. In one episode of his television program *TV Nation*, Moore had a reporter go to the beaches of largely white Greenwich, Connecticut, and bring along some black friends. He did a feature on the Ku Klux Klan, and was involved in a documentary film in the early 1990s that attacked racist militia groups in Michigan.

Moore relentlessly exposes those who fail to meet his standards of racial fairness and equality. For example, only 5 percent of journalists are black. "At work," Moore proclaims, "we whites still get the plum jobs, double the pay, and a seat in the front of the business to happiness and success." Hollywood is another favorite target. Moore complains that he has "never had a meeting at a Hollywood studio with a black executive in charge, never seen a black agent at the film/TV agency that used to represent me."[17] He claims that he was so angry about this that he left his agent. (His new agent is also white, however.)

Hollywood is racist, according to Moore, because there are not enough African-Americans in senior positions. "I now play a game with myself," he wrote in *Stupid White Men*, "trying to clock how long it will be before I spot a black man or woman who isn't wearing a uniform or sitting at a receptionist's desk (they do the Negro-at-the-reception-desk trick in L.A., too). During my last three trips to Los Angeles the clock never stopped: the black head count was zero."[18]

In 1998, Moore proposed initiating what he called a "very strong affirmative action policy regarding gender and race, but especially regarding class." He said he personally wanted to hire minorities "who come from the working class, who do not have a college education, and through these people we will reach a wider audience than the converted."[19] In *Stupid White Men,* he proclaimed his plans to "hire only black people" to help the cause. Pointing his finger at the rest of us, he sermonizes: "If you're white and you really want to change things, why not start with yourself?"

So I decided to do that by starting with . . . Michael Moore. How does he himself fare using the "black head count" method?

First I checked the senior credits for his latest film—*Fahrenheit 911.* In the film itself, he shows army recruiters targeting black youth at a shopping mall and includes clips of black leaders like Reps. Maxine Waters and John Conyers lamenting American racism. Then I checked the list of senior people on the crew: Moore had hired fourteen producers, three editors, a production manager, and a production coordinator. All nineteen are white. So were all three cameramen and the two people who did the original music.[20] I found this odd. Two years earlier, in *Stupid White Men,* he had bragged how his last five employees hired had been black. He had also written, "If you're African-American and you'd like to work in the media . . . then I encourage you to drop me a line and send me your resume." Perhaps they all got lost in the mail.

Obviously, I thought, this must be some sort of anomaly. Michael Moore is too sensitive, too in tune with racism in America, to be so exclusionary. So I checked the credits on his other projects.

Bowling for Columbine: fourteen producers, *thirteen* of them white. The two executives in charge of production:

both white, along with the *cameramen, the film editor, and the music composer.*

The Big One, his 1997 documentary about workers' rights: *five credited producers,* all white, along with *both music composers, two directors of photography, the production manager, and editor.*

Canadian Bacon, his 1995 feature film: *ten producers,* all white, along with *both music composers, two film editors, and the director of photography.*

Pets or Meat: The Return to Flint, his 1992 follow-up documentary to *Roger & Me: three producers,* all white.

Roger & Me, his first documentary, *two producers,* both white.

TV Nation, his television program, which aired on NBC and Fox: *thirteen producers,* all of them white. *Four film editors,* all white, along with *ten writers,* all of whom were white.

The Awful Truth, a television program that ran for several seasons, had *six writers,* all of them white; *seventeen producers, fifteen* of them white; *nine film editors,* all white; *music composer and cinematographer,* both white.

The same pattern applied to the people he hired to help him research and write his books. In his most recent work, *Dude, Where's My Country?,* he credits a brain trust behind the book, three people who did fact checking, and two members from his staff. All seven are white.

In short, of the 134 producers, editors, cinematographers, composers, and production coordinators Moore hired, only three were black. (He did hire one white producer who majored in African-American Studies. Perhaps that counts.)

For those keeping track, Michael Moore comes in well below the 5 percent figure in journalism that he is so exercised about.

As for his alleged commitment to hiring "working-class" people who lack a college education, the vast majority of the senior people he has hired are from Manhattan and Beverly Hills. Almost to a person they are college graduates. The reporters he hired for his television programs included such proletarians as the Oxford-educated son of writer Paul Theroux, a Revlon model, a stockbroker, and an established soap opera actor who went to USC. The producers and writers he's hired are all—with only two exceptions—Hollywood veterans who had worked at *The Late Show with David Letterman,* produced movies and network programs, and attended colleges (some even went to law school). So much for Moore's commitment to affirmative action.

When not denouncing Americans' failure to hire more blacks, Moore points the finger at de facto segregation and white flight as evidence that we are a racist society. Americans might be "magnanimous enough to say, 'Sure you can even live in here in our neighborhood; your kids can go to our kids' school. Why the hell not? We were just leaving anyway.'" Americans "gave black America a pat on the back—and then ran like the devil to the suburbs." All evidence of racism in his mind.[21]

Moore wrote those words from the comfort of his beautiful home in Central Lake, where he has his main residence and spends about two-thirds of his time. An exclusive community in northern Michigan of more than 2,500, about which the 2000 U.S. Census reveals a startling fact: Central Lake is 97.5 percent white, and, amazingly, *not a single African-American lives in the entire town.*

Few evils loom larger for Moore than American corporations. Like his intellectual godfather Noam Chomsky, Moore has spent most of his life trashing them, starting with *Roger & Me* when he skewered General Motors. In *The Big One*, he took on Nike and PayDay candy bars. Violent crime in America is a product of the gun industry, he claimed in *Bowling for Columbine*. Oil companies loom large in *Fahrenheit 911*. On his television programs *TV Nation* and *The Awful Truth*, he attacked HMOs and criticized defense contractors as being part of the military-industrial complex. In his forthcoming film, *Sicko*, he accuses pharmaceutical companies and HMOs of letting Americans die in order to boost their profits. "We need protection from our own multi-millionaire, corporate terrorists," he warns, "the ones who rip off our old-age pensions, destroy the environment, deplete irreplaceable fossil fuels in the name of profit, deny us our rights to universal health care, take people's jobs away whenever the mood hits them."[22] Companies like Halliburton are particularly vile: run by a bunch of "thugs." He told one audience in Great Britain: "I would just like to make a modest proposal: from now on, for every Brit or American kid that's killed in this war, I would like Halliburton to slay one mid-level executive."[23]

Because corporations are so evil, Moore insists on being morally clean by keeping out of the stock market. In *Stupid White Men*, he explains his position: "A couple of years ago I was talking to a guy in a bar who happened to be a stockbroker. He asked me about my 'investments.'

I told him I didn't have any, that I don't own a single share of stock. He was stunned. 'You mean you don't have a portfolio where you keep your money?' 'I don't think it's a good idea to keep your money in portfolios,' I replied, 'or in a briefcase, or even under the futon. I save what little I can in a place called a "bank," where I have what the old-timers call a "savings account." ' "[24] He repeated this claim in a 1997 letter to the online magazine *Salon,* saying, "I don't own any stock."[25] His advice to other Americans was to stay out of the market. "It's Vegas," he told Brian Lamb on *Booknotes.* "That's the rich man's game."[26]

Publicly, Moore claims that he doesn't invest in the stock market out of moral principle. Privately he tells the IRS something completely different. Moore and his wife, Kathleen Glynn, have a private foundation that they established shortly after he started making serious money from *Roger & Me.* The foundation allows them to donate funds tax free, make money on their investments, and give the proceeds to any cause they see fit. Moore and his wife have complete control over the assets; there is no outside manager or trustee. The foundation's registered address is their home in Michigan. Michael Moore signs all the tax forms personally.[27]

The year Moore claimed in *Stupid White Men* that he didn't own any stock, he reported to the IRS that his foundation had more than $280,000 in corporate stock and close to $100,000 in corporate bonds. (These are the investments we know about. He likely has more. According to IRS documents, the allegedly stockless Moore hired a broker at Fleet Financial in Boston, which caters to high-net-worth individuals.)

The IRS forms make for interesting reading. Over the past five years, Moore's "savings account" has included such evil pharmaceutical and medical companies as Pfizer, Merck, Genzyme, Elan PLC, Eli Lilly, Becton Dickinson, and Boston Scientific. "Being screwed by your HMO and ill-served by pharmaceutical companies is a shared American experience," he recently told the *Detroit News*. "The system, inferior to that of much poorer nations, benefits the few at the expense of the many."[28] Count Moore himself as one of those "few." He may savage HMOs in his film *Sicko,* but he has also owned shares of Pharmacia Corporation and Tenet Healthcare. He must have liked their price-to-earnings ratios.

Moore's supposedly nonexistent portfolio also includes big bad energy giants like Sunoco, Noble Energy, Schlumberger, Williams Companies, Transocean Sedco Forex ("the world's largest offshore drilling company"), and Anadarko, all firms that "deplete irreplaceable fossil fuels in the name of profit" as he put it in *Dude, Where's My Country?* And in perhaps the ultimate irony, he also has owned shares in Halliburton. According to IRS filings, Moore sold Halliburton for a 15 percent profit and bought shares in Noble, Ford, General Electric (another defense contractor), AOL Time Warner (evil corporate media), and McDonald's (well-known despoiler of the Amazon, bad-will ambassador abroad, and purveyor of American obesity). Also on Moore's investment menu: defense contractors Honeywell, Boeing, and Loral. A look at the tax return he filed in 2002 makes it clear why he's so bitter about those corporate scandals and CEO greed. He bought almost $12,000 worth of WorldCom stock in 1999, only to see it lose almost 90 percent of its value.

For a man who claims to support labor unions and has attacked Nike for using underpaid Third World workers, it's striking how few of the companies he owns shares in have unions themselves. Most of them are high-tech firms that outsource production to China, or major oil conglomerates that do business in the developing world. I couldn't find a single investment that involved a heavily unionized company.

This is quite a portfolio for a man who claims that he has no portfolio and does not consider capitalism okay "on any level."[29]

Moore likes to boast about his foundation. In his 2003 interview with Brian Lamb, he said, "We have a foundation that we've set up, where we help out a lot of first-time filmmakers. We also fund a lot of things in the Flint area and a lot of social action groups and things like that. I'm a dangerous guy to give a lot of money to, for money falls in my lap like this, you know, because I have so few material wants, you know, other than my fine wardrobe."[30] He also told the *New Yorker* that the foundation funds "first-time filmmakers, battered women's shelters, and soup kitchens, among other things."[31]

Once again, his filing with the IRS tells a different story. Yes, there were a few modest grants to programs helping the poor—but nothing on the scale he likes to brag about. For a man who by 2002 had a net worth in eight figures, he gave away a modest $36,000 through the foundation, much of it to his friends in the film business or tony cultural organizations that later provided him with venues to promote his books and films. Indeed, he gave away just barely the minimum necessary to maintain the foundation's charitable status.

In 2000, for example, he handed out just $22,000 in grants. Of that amount, $4,500 went to that most proletarian of organizations, the Film Society of Lincoln Center in New York, and another $1,000 went to the Ann Arbor Film Festival, which both held lavish events that helped promote *Bowling for Columbine*. The next year he gave $2,500 to Pamela Yates, who was a producer for his NBC program *TV Nation*, and made another grant to his friend Jeff Gibbs, who provided the music for *Bowling for Columbine* and helped write some of his books. He has also given money to the New York Video Festival, which held events promoting his television show *TV Nation*. In 2002, $25,000 went to the American Library Association, which is particularly interesting given that Moore credits ALA members with getting HarperCollins to reconsider a decision to cancel his anti-Bush screed *Stupid White Men* after 9/11. He also sent $1,000 to Greater Manchester Against Wars, a British protest group that does not enjoy tax-exempt status in the United States. How he claimed this contribution as "charitable" remains a mystery.

He further saw fit to use the foundation, which was established to promote issues relating to "the economy, class issues, the poor, women, war and peace, race and labor," to fund environmental projects like the Grass River

Natural Area and the GTRLC Loon Nursery. Both work to preserve wildlife and natural settings around Torch Lake, no doubt helping to maintain his property values.

Moore has also been selective in his corporate targets. In late 2004, for example, an enormously profitable company (net profits over $200 million) was rolling in dough. But instead of giving bonuses to the worker bees, execs were laying off 65 of 485 employees. When the PayDay candy bar company had done this before, in the 1990s, Moore showed up with a camera crew and pointed a mike in the CEO's face, accusing him of firing people for doing too good a job. This time the CEOs fired their employees and Michael Moore never showed up. Why? The execs were Bob and Harvey Weinstein, who distribute Moore's movies. He picked these same execs to fund and help distribute his next film, *Sicko*.[32]

In his book *Downsize This*, Moore proudly parades his commitment to labor unions. In the introduction he says that he hired two researchers for the book and encouraged them to join a union. "Now, I know, you're saying, 'Hey, Mike, your workers don't need a union! I'll bet your office is a really cool place to work, a nonstop rock-n-roll party for the proletariat!' Right, except for one thing: they do not own this book, will not share in its potential profits, must work long hours, and can be let go at any time."[33] In 1996, Moore proclaimed that "all places of employment should have unions. All workers need representation unless they are owners of the company. That is my given philosophy."[34]

That may be his philosophy, but it's not necessarily his practice. Moore loves unions and paying union wages if it's on someone else's dime. But when it affects his own bottom line, you'd better hope he doesn't outsource you.

During the production of *TV Nation* for NBC, Moore called two of the show's writers into his office. They were not members of the Writers Guild and were not receiving health care benefits or a portion of the profits from video sales or reruns. They were planning on joining the union, but said that Moore tried to dissuade them. Eric Zicklin, an associate producer on the show, recalls, "Michael said, 'I'm getting a lot of heat from the union to call you guys writers and pay you under the union rules. I don't have the budget for that. But if they keep coming down on me that'll mean I'll only be able to afford one of you and the other one's gotta go.' "

"He wanted to let us know that this would hurt us if it continued," says Zicklin. "We were scared out of our minds. It was like a theme from *Roger & Me.*"

Randy Cohen, a co-executive producer, says that Moore did not want to give writers proper credit, thereby avoiding having to share the profits. On several occasions the writers had to seek help from the Writers Guild. Says Vito Turso, a spokesman for the Guild, the writers' union "had to arbitrate several complaints from *TV Nation* writers who hadn't received proper payments for their work."[35]

If he can't dissuade people from joining a union, he might just head north to Canada for cheaper wages, a common practice that the L.A. County Labor Federation says is leading to the "wholesale destruction of the Hollywood jobs base." But that hasn't stopped Moore from following suit. Enticed by the Ontario Film Commission, which points to a cheaper Canadian dollar and a provincial tax credit totaling 27 percent of domestic labor costs, Moore has spent quite a bit of money up north. For his film *Canadian Bacon,* he filmed scenes that allegedly took place in the United States in Ontario. The so-called Hacker Factory, for example, where an American industrialist was filmed plotting a war, was actually in Hamilton, Ontario. Scenes involving rapids in Niagara Falls, New York, were also shot in Ontario. Some of the action sequences, which were supposed to take place in the United States, were actually shot in Toronto.

Likewise, the expensive postproduction work for his television program *The Awful Truth* was not done in L.A. or New York, but in Halifax, Nova Scotia. Much of the work and filming in *Bowling for Columbine* was done in Sarnia, Ontario, and Toronto and Windsor.

Publicly, Michael Moore is a populist crusader who stands up to profit-minded corporations on behalf of workers, women, minorities, and the environment. Privately, he is the consummate capitalist single-mindedly focused on money. John Pierson, who distributed *Roger & Me,* found him impossible to deal with. Moore would upbraid him for how much he was making on the film and tell him to share. Pierson could get him to shut up only by pointing out that Moore made more than anyone and should perhaps part with some of his own money.[36] Veteran Hollywood manager Douglas Urbanski used to manage Michael Moore. "He is more money obsessed than any I have known," he says, "and that's saying a lot."[37]

When it comes to spitting out criticism, Moore is like a howitzer: explosive shell follows explosive shell. His claims explode on the American public square and the smoke is visible around the world. Racist, greedy, exploitative, uncaring, criminal: These are labels that he merrily affixes to whomever he chooses. By doing so, he has amassed a considerable fortune and become the newest icon of the international Left. Perhaps his next film will be about an enormously wealthy and cynical filmmaker who does the very things that he accuses others of doing. Naaaaaah. Why not keep a good thing going?

▶▶ *AL FRANKEN*

Habitual Liar,
Mean-Spirited Partisan,
and Racial Discriminator

Noam Chomsky celebrates socialism. Michael Moore bashes corporations. What about Al Franken?

Franken is the latest icon of liberalism. In this new era of perplexity for liberals, the comedian and best-selling author has suddenly become a power broker and an influential analyst. He has been both a friend and an adviser to President Bill Clinton, Sen. Hillary Clinton, and Vice President Al Gore. One writer called him the "Democratic Messiah."[1] Paul Begala, the former Clinton adviser, said, "Al has become a rallying point for Democrats."[2]

Often when he attends political events, he's the largest draw. At a Kerry campaign rally in Nashua, New Hampshire, in early 2004, the senator was greeted by a boisterous crowd. Then Ted Kennedy appeared, to equally strong applause. But when Franken appeared, the *New York Times* reported, "an actual shriek went up—the sort of girl-squeal you associate with footage of the early Beatles."[3] When Kerry was sinking in the polls early in the Democratic primary, Franken called his friends in the media and held a get-together with Kerry so they could get to know him up close. He has floated the possibility of running for the Senate in his home state of Minnesota, and his former writing partner Tom Davis avers that he has even higher ambitions—the presidency itself.

In the 1990s, Franken characterized himself as a "mushy moderate," not strongly committed to the liberal cause, but somewhere in the middle. Now the host of a nationally syndicated radio show on the left-wing Air America, he calls himself a "proud liberal" and a champion of every liberal cause from affirmative action to soak-the-rich taxes. But Franken has become the new rock star of liberalism less because of what he likes than because of what (or whom) he hates.

Specifically, Franken hates conservatives. Tony Perkins, head of the conservative Family Research Council, recalls that when he ran into the commentator at the Republican National Convention, he told Franken that he had been his favorite star on *Saturday Night Live*, "something my conservative friends would probably prefer I not admit to." Franken told Perkins that he had very dangerous ideas, then turned on his heel and walked away.[4]

At a black-tie dinner in Washington, Franken went up to Bush adviser Karl Rove and said, "I'm Al Franken. I hate you and you hate me." Rove was shocked. "I said, 'I haven't met you. You seem like a nice enough fellow, sorry to disappoint you but I don't hate you.' "[5]

Franken has made a specialty out of launching immature and mean-spirited attacks on conservatives. Rather than engage with their ideas, he delights in baiting and taunting his political opponents. Shortly after it was revealed that Franken's nemesis Rush Limbaugh had an addiction to the prescription drug OxyContin, he remarked that Limbaugh would never make it through a twelve-step program because it would require honesty. He called Bill O'Reilly a liar to his face at the Chicago Book Expo in June 2003; and, rather than debate their differences, he clownishly challenged *National Review* editor Rich Lowry to a fistfight. He's made cracks about Sen. Bob Dole's war injury and bad-mouthed Sen. John McCain, a bona fide war hero who spent years in a North Vietnamese POW camp.[6] "Anybody could get captured," Franken said at a Washington dinner. "Essentially, he sat out the war." (When he heard some boos, he continued, "Well, isn't the idea to capture the other guys?") At another Washington dinner, Franken made a tasteless joke about the menstrual cycle of one of Newt Gingrich's daughters.

All this from a man who says that conservatives are "spreading filth, sleaze, and bile through the media apparatus." Franken doesn't so much argue with conservatives as call them names, to the delight of his left-leaning audience. Indeed, his whole modus operandi can be described as one long, snide, ad hominem attack. Conservatives are "extremely mean and nasty," Franken says.[7] They lie, distort, manipulate, preach hate, and generally appeal to people's "dark side." Franken maintains that conservatives alone are responsible for today's polarized political climate.[8]

Franken, with his jokes and insults, wants to change all that: "My grandiose vision is to change the dialogue in this country."[9] Piously, he says that "we have to be civil to each other." And he promises to be the liberal avenger and truth-teller. "Anybody who deliberately propagandizes with lies should be held up to scorn and ridicule."[10] Another one of his high-toned statements: "People have a right to speak out, but they don't have a right to lie or smear."[11] Unlike conservatives, he says, "I do have a sense of decency."[12]

Franken also claims that, unlike his opponents, he lives up to a high ethical standard. "I'm not observant [religiously], but it depends on what practicing your faith means, really, because my parents always taught me that being Jewish was being ethical. So I try to do that. And feeling that justice is about doing what's just. It's something I've taught my kids."[13]

But even those closest to Franken are forced to admit that he often goes too far. One of these old friends is Norman Ornstein, the respected scholar at the American Enterprise Institute. "I have a genuine disdain for Michael Moore, and sometimes Al veers off in that direction," Ornstein remarks. Even lefties like Jeff Blodgett of Minnesota's Wellstone Action admits: "Sometimes he's over the top."[14]

Conservatives have in the past tended to be friendly to Franken, despite their political differences. As described in his book *Lies and the Lying Liars Who Tell Them*, they frequently return his phone calls and are cordial when they meet him. Though the film he wrote, *When a Man Loves a Woman*, was trashed by the *New York Times*, *National Review* gave it a glowing write-up. Franken himself admits that throughout the 1990s, most of his speeches were given before conservative or corporate audiences who paid him to rib conservatives. When he attended the White House correspondents' annual dinners, it was often as the guest of conservative publications like the *Washington Times*. But Franken has not returned the kindness. In addition to making increasingly hysterical attacks, he has left a trail of people who believe they have been deceived when they responded to him with courtesy. For example, when he called an acquaintance, former Minnesota congressman Vin Weber, to chat, he didn't tell him he was interviewing him for a book. He then pulled statements from the conversation and quoted him in *Lies*. In another instance, Franken ran into writer John Fund of the *Wall Street Journal*. According to Franken, Fund told him that much of what he had written about Rush Limbaugh in a previous book was true, and he reported that in *Lies*. "It's simply not true," says Fund, who said they made a little small talk. "In the future, I simply will say nothing for fear that anything I will say will be misrepresented." Paul Gigot, editor of the *Wall Street Journal,* says that he was similarly treated by Franken.

Franken says that conservatives use "unfair mean" jokes while he uses "fair mean" jokes. (He chooses not to define his terms.)[15] In his defense, he also says, "I'm making fun of the meanness in public debate by being mean myself." But the fact is that Franken has always been nasty and brutish (the fact that he is also short should not be held against him). If conservatives had uttered anything remotely close to some of the things he has said, there would be universal outrage.

Franken's style of angry humor has early biographical roots. According to Franken, it all began in second grade. After girls in his class put on "this really insipid show, 'I'm a little teapot,' I sat down and wrote a scathing parody. I got the other boys together, and we dressed in drag. The girls were in tears. That made it a success."[16] When he got older, Franken attended an elite prep school outside of Minneapolis. Then it was on to Harvard. He was never asked to join Harvard's Hasty Pudding Club, the humorous dramatic society, and it obviously left a bitter mark. Here's what Franken told the *Harvard Crimson* when he was writing for *Saturday Night Live:* "I just don't like homosexuals. If you ask me, they're all homosexuals in the Pudding. Hey, I was glad when that Pudding homosexual got killed in Philadelphia."[17] It was a reference to the death of a Harvard grad in that city. Imagine if a conservative had said such a thing.

After college, Franken landed a job as a writer on *Saturday Night Live,* where he would work off and on from 1975 to 1995. (He left after producers refused to give him the anchor slot on the weekend news update parody.) While on the show he wrote a skit about policemen who shoot homosexuals. The skit was criticized by groups who wanted to know what was so funny about killing homosexuals. Producers didn't revive it. Another idea Franken had was to air a talk show about people who wanted to assassinate Ted Kennedy. When the producer sat down with Franken and his partner to discuss the idea, he said, "I don't believe you guys wrote this. Usually, when I see things you write they're at least funny, but I don't see what's funny about this."

Nevertheless, Franken quickly became a key figure in the *SNL* writing shop and soon started appearing on-air. Fellow *SNL* writer Dave Mandell, who was hired by Franken, said that part of the secret to Franken's success was "he's not afraid to be ugly."[18] Franken pushed one sketch called "What's My Addiction?" in which a panel would ask a group of drugged-out addicts which drugs they were hooked on. Then there was Franken's "breast cancer" skit. A man laments that his wife has only one breast after cancer surgery and can't stand to have sex with her.[19] "Al Franken has really gone over the edge this time," one of the producers said. Pushing the envelope even further, Franken submitted comedy material based on the Holocaust—but it never made it on the air.[20]

Some of the skits that Franken and the team came up with were downright racist, according to writers Doug Hill and Jeff Weingrad in their extensive history of *SNL*. In one sketch, Garrett Morris, the sole black performer on the show at the time, was supposed to do a parody commercial for a toothpaste called "Tarbrush," which darkened blacks' white shiny teeth. Two black technicians walked off the show in protest.[21]

Franken also apparently took great pride in making sure that Henry Kissinger's son couldn't get tickets to *Saturday Night Live*—years after the Vietnam War—because he was upset with his father's Vietnam policies.[22]

After leaving *SNL*, Franken suddenly emerged as a partisan culture warrior with a book called *Rush Limbaugh Is a Big Fat Idiot.* At the time, he defended it as a fair book. (He later admitted that "the Rush book was a liberal screed. I meant it to be a political act.")[23] He made numerous fat jokes (thirty-seven on one page), said that Reagan adviser Lyn Nofziger looked like a pornographer, called Sen. Phil Gramm "mammario-fetishistic," and imagined a homosexual affair between Pat Buchanan and Dan Quayle. When he was asked to pick the winner of the 1996 Super Bowl, he said, "I don't know who is going to win, but during halftime, Rush will eat three Domino's pizzas, two bags of pork rinds, twelve Ding Dongs, and wash it all down with two 2-liter bottles of Diet Coke."[24]

Franken claimed that Rush himself was to blame for these attacks because he was so mean. But Franken was simply doing what he had always done, putting people down and making fun of them, whether they were breast cancer survivors, drug addicts, homosexuals, or conservative talk show hosts.

His favorite example of Limbaugh's "meanness" is a single sketch done on Rush's television show in 1993, shortly after Clinton took office. Limbaugh put up a picture of Socks the cat and said, "Did you know that the Clintons not only have a White House cat, but they also have a White House dog?" A picture of a teenaged Chelsea Clinton then appeared, looking especially gawky with her frizzy hair and braces. No doubt this probably ought not to have aired. But it infuriated Franken, who mentioned the sketch in his Rush Limbaugh book, his *Lies* book, and in dozens of speech appearances. He even confronted talk show host Sean Hannity in the Fox News Channel green room because he wanted him to "admit that Rush deliberately insulted a thirteen-year-old." As Hannity tells it, security had to be called because Franken was so obnoxious.

Yet back in 1993, when Franken was a producer and lead writer for *SNL*, they did *two* skits that featured a homely teenaged Chelsea Clinton. In one she was compared unfavorably to the glamorous Gore daughters; in another, Julia Sweeney dressed up as Chelsea, wearing braces, a frizzy wig, and pimples in what one biographer called "a devastating send-up of Chelsea."[25]

Franken does this all the time, pontificating about some outrage by conservatives, only to turn out to have done something worse himself, and with more gusto. Consider the scandal involving the abuse of Iraqi prisoners at Abu Ghraib. On Air America he has gleefully ripped the Bush administration, declaring the prison abuse a disgrace and demanding that Secretary of Defense Donald Rumsfeld be held accountable. On the Air America blog, his show went after Rush Limbaugh after the talk show host compared some of what had happened at Abu Ghraib with acts of college hazing. But here's what Franken had said a little more than a year earlier at the National Press Club: "Here's a tool that I think we should consider keeping on the table—torture. I'm talking about the detainees. We have like three hundred detainees—not all the detainees, by the way—just like the guy who had an apartment in Paterson, New Jersey, and who was inquiring about crop-dusting. That guy knows something— right? Now, you know that he's willing to die for this perverse cause. My question is: Is he willing to take a— poker up the butt for it? You know he wants to service the seventy-two virgins in paradise. Does he think he can do that after we have crushed his testicles?"[26] Imagine the outcry if Rush Limbaugh or Ann Coulter had uttered those hyperbolic sentiments. What would Franken say to that?

In *Lies and the Lying Liars Who Tell Them,* Franken gallantly defended liberal women whom he claims were attacked by Coulter in a column on the issue of conservative women being insulted for their appearance. Coulter made the point that conservative women like Katherine Harris (of Florida recount fame) and Linda Tripp were constantly being mocked and laughed at because of their makeup or looks. But there were never such attacks on people like Madeleine Albright, Maxine Waters, or Janet Reno. Coulter never attacked these women, of course. She just declared that there was a double standard in their treatment by the liberal media. Franken affected to be outraged, claiming that Coulter had indirectly "point[ed] to five supposedly unattractive Democratic women."[27] Yet only a few years earlier, Franken himself had stood up in front of a large Washington audience and cracked that Janet Reno was so unattractive she would have trouble getting $25 for a lap dance.

In addition to being the arbiter of taste and decency, Franken proclaims himself to be the singular bearer of truth, and famously insists that conservatives are habitual liars. Here are some examples of what Franken considers "lies." The first few involve disputes about facts. In the national debate over President Bush's tax cuts, for example, Franken said that more money went to upper-income taxpayers, while Bush said lower-income taxpayers received proportionally bigger cuts. Franken calls Bush a liar, and that is supposedly the end of it. In other instances he cites sources like columnist Paul Krugman and the Pew Charitable Trusts to dispute facts from the Heritage Foundation or the Office of Management and Budget. In these factual disputes, conservatives are again described as liars. In other instances, he highlights misstatements of fact and declares the people who said them to be liars. Thus he criticized Dick Cheney for declaring that he saw "row upon row of crosses" at Arlington National Cemetery when he should have said headstones. When Ann Coulter said that *Newsweek* editor Evan Thomas's father was socialist Norman Thomas, Franken called her a "liar" because Norman was actually Evan's grandfather.[28] Much of Franken's best-selling book includes this kind of material.

Most famously, Franken went after Fox News host Bill O'Reilly over awards that were won by his previous show, *Inside Edition*. O'Reilly had said that the program won a "Peabody Award" when he meant to say "Polk." (Both are prestigious journalism prizes, easily confused.) At his now famous confrontation with O'Reilly at the American Booksellers Convention in Chicago, Franken declared that he was a liar. O'Reilly in turn took him to task for claiming to be an unbiased truth-teller: "Even people who agree with you in this room, they can't possibly think that you're objective. . . . You make a nice living being a propagandist, and more power to you, but don't put yourself up as a truth-teller, because you're not." Franken's comeback: "I am, though . . . I do tell the truth."[29]

"Telling the truth is something I take seriously," he

wrote in *Lies,* "and I try to hold myself to an impossibly high standard."[30]

Consider this, however. When Franken wrote *Lies and the Lying Liars Who Tell Them,* he was a fellow at Harvard University. To research the book, he organized a study group made up of students to assist him. He sent word out on campus and received numerous applications. How many did he get? Franken gives two widely different answers. He told the *Harvard Crimson* that he received 90 applications to join his study group, but writes in *Lies* that he received 700.[31] It's hard to see how you can confuse 90 with 700. Does this make him a liar? It's a lot easier to understand someone confusing a Polk with a Peabody.

In *Lies,* Franken makes all sorts of errors that are much more grievous than anything his conservative "liars" have done. He claims, for example, that Bill O'Reilly's mother told the *Washington Post* that the family regularly took vacations in Florida, a sure sign that O'Reilly didn't have the modest upbringing that he claimed. But the article that Franken cites (Paul Farhi, "The Life of O'Reilly," *Washington Post,* December 13, 2000) says nothing of the sort. Similarly, Franken writes that Sen. Max Cleland had three limbs blown off by a "V.C. grenade" while in Vietnam. Actually the tragedy was a result of a training accident, as Cleland writes in his memoir.[32] Franken further asserts that the General Accounting Office refutes Bush administration claims that there was "no record of damage" done by Clinton staffers to the White House before they left the building. Actually the report begins, "Damage, theft, vandalism, and pranks occurred in the White House complex during the 2001 presidential transition."

Elsewhere Franken claims that Assistant Secretary of State Richard Armitage was so mad after a meeting on Capitol Hill that he knocked veteran reporter Helen Thomas to the ground, breaking her hip and jaw. Thomas says the incident never happened.[33]

Franken says that lies must be exposed. Yet somehow he could never bring himself to criticize the only American president ever impeached for lying under oath. To the contrary, Franken boasts that he is in "Bill Clinton's pocket" and calls him the greatest president of his lifetime.

The fact is, Franken uses lies (he calls them "ruses") all the time. For example, for his book he wrote letters to Attorney General John Ashcroft and twenty-eight others in which he baldly misrepresented himself:

"I am currently a fellow at Harvard's Kennedy School of Government, where I am working on a book about abstinence programs in our public schools entitled 'Savin' It!'

". . . The book's fourth chapter, 'Role Modelin' It!,' will feature the personal stories of abstinence heroes for our nation's young people to emulate. . . .

"I would very much appreciate it if you could share your abstinence story. So far, I have received wonderful testimonies from HHS Secretary Tommy Thompson, William J. Bennett, White House Press Secretary Ari Fleischer, Cardinal Egan, Senator Rick Santorum, and National Security Adviser Condoleezza Rice. (I'm still hoping to hear back from the President!)"

Of course this was a tasteless joke and no one fell for it. (For those keeping track of such things, Franken sent at least one of his children to a private New York school that boasts an "abstinence plus" sex ed curriculum.)[34] When Harvard found out about his prank, they were not amused. "You could call it irony, I call it bad judgment," said Alex Jones, director of Harvard's Shorenstein Center. Franken was forced to apologize. Jones continued to insist, however, that Franken's *Lies* was a "serious" book.[35]

Next, Franken wanted to slam the fundamentalist Christian college Bob Jones University, so he asked one of his research assistants to apply to the South Carolina school and then traveled to visit the campus with him. What they were looking for was damning material revealing how racist, bigoted, and nutty the school is.

The deception lasted for only a few minutes before the plot was uncovered. Franken is forced to admit that they were still treated nicely, even though they were caught lying to college officials.

Another of his favorite themes is that conservatives are "racists."[36] When he gives corporate speeches, he begins by saying, "Looking out at your faces today, I can see that this group hasn't caved in to that whole affirmative action nonsense." According to Franken, the audiences "look around, see all the white faces, and laugh." "Most of the time, they burst out laughing right away."[37] In Franken's view, the political issue is simple: Republicans "hurt black people and help rich people. Who tend, again generally, to be white." He likes to say that the dearth of African-Americans in the Republican Party is a sign of racism and that conservatives are hostile to "diversity." The Republican Party is the home of "Southern bigots," but they "aren't just racist in the South."[38]

Writing in the *Los Angeles Times,* he accused Republicans of "race-baiting" and chided them for being unconcerned about the black unemployment crisis. Racism is rampant in America, and he cites the fact that employers don't hire blacks precisely because they are black.[39]

Once again, however, while Franken loves to point a moralistic finger at conservatives, he has trouble facing the same sort of scrutiny.

In 1992, Franken gave a speech at Harvard; four hundred students and faculty crowded in to listen. Among those in attendance was a young student named Teja Arboleda. After a few softball questions about then-president George H. W. Bush, Arboleda stood up and asked: "As a producer and the head writer of the series, what do you plan to do to represent minorities and women more justly on your program [*Saturday Night Live*]?"

Franken was caught flat-footed; there was a pause. "Well," he drawled laconically, "I'm looking for a couple of Blaacks. . . . I am looking for a couple of Hispaanics, oh and I'm looking for a couple of gaaaays. . . . "

Half the audience laughed, the other half booed. Arboleda continued, "Well, let's put it this way. How many minorities do you have as writers on your show?"

"Ah," said Franken, adjusting his glasses, without answering.

"Okay . . . well, how many women do you have as writers?"

"Ah . . . two, but they don't get paid to be writers." Women began hissing and, according to Arboleda, who later wrote a book about growing up in a multiracial society, "Mr. Franken became visibly upset." After the crowd simmered down, he took more questions. He made a few more jokes ("minorities aren't funny") and would occasionally look into the audience and ask, "Oh, where's that ethnic guy?"[40]

It's easy to see why Franken stumbled over Arboleda's question. For a guy who loves roasting corporations (and Republicans) for their lack of commitment to "diversity" and apparent "racism," it's hard to find a single example of Franken hiring an African-American to do much of anything.

At Air America (at least at the time of this writing), Franken had two executive producers and four researchers—every one of them white. When Franken wrote *Lies* at Harvard, he selected 14 undergrads and graduate students to be research assistants. From a pool of 700 (or 90, depending on which Franken account you believe), he personally conducted two rounds of interviews. Of all those hundreds (or dozens) of applicants, he apparently couldn't find one qualified member of a minority to join "Team Franken." All fourteen of his researchers were white. The research assistants on his previous books were also white. Likewise, all the senior people (director, writers, producers, and those who handled the musical score, editing, and cinematography) in his feature film *Stuart Saves His Family* were white. His 2004 documentary, *Fox vs. Franken,* had eleven senior people, all of whom were white. The full crew for *The Al Franken Show* launched in 2004 on the Sundance Channel included five producers, all of them white. He produced three specials for *Saturday Night Live* ("Presidential Bash 1992," "Saturday Night Live Goes Commercial," and "Fifteenth Anniversary Special"); all of the senior people were white. On his film *When a Man Loves a Woman*, all of the producers, the director, and other senior administrative people were white, as they were for his 1986 picture *One More Saturday Night*. His short-lived television series *Lateline* (which he starred in and created) included twenty-five senior slots; all but one were held by whites. From his days at *Saturday Night Live*, I found plenty of white writers who credit Franken with hiring them, but have yet to find a single black writer.

Do we detect a pattern here?

In total, we are talking about 112 people whom Franken either hired directly or had a strong influence in determining whether they would work on a project. *Only one was black.* What this means, of course, is that Al Franken's staff is actually whiter than Bob Jones University (which manages a 1 percent black enrollment), a school that Franken labels "racist."

Franken has insisted over the years that the lack of diversity among Republicans and conservatives is a proof of latent racism. What can be said about the similar lack of diversity among Franken's own employees?

Though Franken started as a comedy writer, he now says that he wants to be taken seriously as a political commentator and even a potential Senate candidate. But it's not his comedy background that hinders him; it's his hypocrisy. Imagine if a conservative had made cracks about former senator Max Cleland the way Franken does about Bob Dole's war injury; or if an editor at *National Review* had told a newspaper reporter that he was glad a homosexual was murdered; or if a conservative talk show host made a tasteless joke about Chelsea Clinton's menstrual cycle. Franken and a lot of other people would be outraged.

I tried to get Franken to talk to me about the yawning gap between his advocacy of affirmative action and his glaring failure to engage in it himself. He is familiar with my work. I've appeared on Air America to defend my recent book on the Bushes, and he mentioned it on his radio program. I left messages for him through two producers and wrote a letter to his home address. The man who once challenged Rich Lowry to a fistfight hasn't been heard from.

▶▶ *TED KENNEDY*

Environmental Rapist, Tax Cheat, and Oil Profiteer

Ted Kennedy is one of the great liberal lions of the U.S. Senate. For the past forty years, no one in that body has roared louder for liberal causes. Name the issue and Kennedy has been there: Soak the rich with higher taxes; abortion on demand; protect the planet from ecological damage; take on the wealthy and polluting oil companies; universal health care for all Americans; ban most guns. If there is a battle to be waged, Kennedy is usually in the middle of it. And unlike many of his Senate colleagues, Kennedy is not one to back down.

While people like Chomsky, Moore, and Franken have been battling from outside the system, Kennedy has been pushing their agenda from the inside. Many of today's most prominent liberals see Kennedy as a role model. Both Bill and Hillary Clinton have proclaimed him to be one of their heroes, as have Al Gore, John Kerry, and a generation of liberal activists. Ralph Nader has often found Kennedy's Senate staff supportive of his efforts, and environmentalist groups heap awards on him and regard him as a "visionary." Many on the left believe that were it not for that unfortunate night at Chappaquiddick, Kennedy would have been president.

No doubt much of the liberal love for Kennedy comes from his air of moral certitude. With fine senatorial bombast he skewers his opponents, frequently calling their motives into question. Republicans like Reagan and George W. Bush protect the rich while he protects the poor; the wealthy try to avoid paying taxes while he wants to hold them to pay their fair share; corporations pollute the earth while he is a lone sentinel protecting the environment; Americans with guns are dangerous and he wants to rein them in.

But do his actions match his words? Does Kennedy actually live by the principles he so loudly and vigorously proclaims? A closer look at his conduct in private life reveals that this champion of liberal causes is really the king of liberal hypocrites.

Perhaps no other issue has captured Kennedy's attention more than taxes. Pick any decade of his public life and you will find the same message: The government should take from the rich and give to the poor. He seems particularly offended by the use of loopholes and tax shelters by the rich. On the Senate floor he said he wanted to see to it "that the word 'shelter' disappears from the tax vocabulary." On another occasion he rose to say, "Instead of shutting down classrooms, let us shut off tax shelters."

He clearly sees such income redistribution as a moral imperative. When he introduces a tax increase, he claims he is "fighting for working Americans," while tax cuts mean in Kennedy-speak "giveaways" and "bonanzas" for the rich. Implicit in this view is the idea that all this money doesn't really belong to its owners but to the government. Repealing a tax cut is therefore a way for the government to "save" money. What he means by the "rich" may also surprise you. He recently proposed repealing Bush tax cuts for any household making more than $130,000 a year.

Kennedy's other great tax cause in recent years has been supporting the estate or inheritance tax. Permanently repealing this tax, as President Bush wants to do, would "benefit millionaires" and hurt the poor. What could be more gallant—more in the tradition of FDR— than a rich man who defends the inheritance tax?

The Kennedy family, of course, earns considerably more than $130,000 per year (estimates put the family's net worth at around $500 million). What's more, few have been as effective at avoiding taxes than this tax-hiking, free-spending clan.

Take the family's real estate investments, for example. By far the largest crown jewel in the Kennedy crown was Merchandise Mart, a Chicago real estate company that Joe Kennedy started in 1935. Over the course of six decades, Merchandise Mart expanded and was eventually sold in 1998 with another real estate trust for $625 million.

But Merchandise Mart is not your typical company. In 1947, Joe Kennedy divided its ownership among family members and put it in the form of a trust. The trust was not set up in their home state of Massachusetts, New York, Florida, or even California. This trust wasn't even domiciled in the United States. Instead the Kennedy trust was set up in ... *Fiji.*

There is no evidence that any member of the Kennedy clan had ever been to that far-off Pacific Island or could even locate it on a map. But what Fiji did bring them was the possibility of avoiding scrutiny by the IRS and federal authorities.[1]

Through an intricate web of trusts and private foundations, they have kept most of the family pie from ever ending up in the hands of the IRS. Thus when Joe Kennedy died, the family's fortune was acknowledged to be between $300 million and $500 million. But they paid just $134,330.90 in estate taxes.[2] For those keeping score, the effective inheritance tax they paid was approximately .04 percent, assuming the lower figure of $300 million. Given the probable size of the Kennedy fortune, the actual savings was undoubtedly much higher.

To put this audacious dodge in perspective, consider how the current inheritance tax system works—the one that Kennedy has called "equitable and just." The current tax rate is 49 percent on any money passed to your children after the first $2 million (it is slowly going up to track with inflation). In other words, a farmer or small businessman worth $2.26 million, who didn't have the benefit of Kennedy tax shelters and foreign-based trusts, would pay the same amount in estate taxes as the Kennedys did on their entire half-billion-dollar fortune.

Much of the Kennedy fortune is still in trusts today,

which are structured to keep the family from paying higher taxes. Ted Kennedy receives nice checks every year from trusts set up in 1926, 1936, 1978, 1987, and 1997.[3]

Sometimes you don't need a trust to get a tax cut; political influence will do just as well. In 1980, an investigation by the *Chicago Tribune* revealed that Merchandise Mart had avoided paying millions of dollars in property taxes. While the property in question was worth $35 million, the tax assessor had set the value at $22.8 million, far below that of smaller properties in less desirable areas. As a result, the Kennedys paid $4 million less in taxes than they should have over the course of two years. Another Kennedy building, Apparel Mart, got the same treatment, saving the family millions more in taxes. Remember Ted Kennedy's concern about schools being shut down because of tax shelters? These millions in real estate taxes would have gone to Chicago public schools. Instead, they remained in the Kennedy family trust.

Thomas Tully, tax assessor for Cook County, Chicago, was a Kennedy political ally. The senator had flown in several times to host fund-raising dinners for Tully when he was up for reelection. After Tully left office, the Democrat tax assessor who followed him raised the assessments. Soon after, a federal grand jury was empaneled to investigate reports that Tully had become wealthy while in office through real estate deals with developers, like the Kennedys, whose taxes he cut. Tully was never charged and since 1980 has been a regular political contributor to the Kennedys, giving thousands to no less than four different family members running for office.[4] The Kennedys never did give the millions back to Chicago's public schools.

In his financial disclosure forms, we find that Ted Kennedy has a large appetite for tax-free Massachusetts bonds, putting hundreds of thousands of dollars into investments that allow him to avoid paying state taxes on his profits. This penchant for tax avoidance seems to be contagious. In 2004, Kennedy's father-in-law, Edmund Reggie, a former member of the Democratic National Committee, settled a lawsuit with the IRS and agreed to pay $800,000. Reggie had apparently tried to shift real estate assets into his wife's name to avoid paying back taxes.[5]

Ted Kennedy yields to no one in his zeal for affirmative action. He favors racial set-asides on federal contracts, ensuring that minority businesses get a guaranteed portion of contracts. He favors affirmative action both in businesses and in school admissions. Yet once again, where his family's private interests are concerned, the family's crusade for racial justice fades from view.

In 1981 the Kennedy family created two limited partnerships—WDC Associates and Fourth and D Street Partners—to buy a prime piece of real estate in Washington, D.C. WDC Associates was made up of Senator Kennedy and his siblings (the senator's personal investment was $308,000). Fourth and D Street was made up of the next generation of the family, including Rep. Joseph P. Kennedy II. But there was one problem. The D.C. Redevelopment Land Agency had a minority clause, which required minority-owned-business participation in any development project. This affirmative action set-aside was obligingly waived by Washington mayor Marion Berry, a longtime political ally of Senator Kennedy, who in turn was very influential in determining how much federal money went into the District of Columbia. The Kennedys were allowed to purchase an entire city block encompassing Fourth and Fifth Streets and D and E Streets S.E., just blocks from the Capitol Building, for $3 million in a no-bid deal. There was no minority-business participation in the project.

This purchase was the start of a very lucrative enterprise for the Kennedy family. With the property so close to the Capitol Building, and with the federal government aggressively looking for office space, over the course of the next decade the family converted the city block–sized property into an upscale office complex. The federally funded subway system conveniently put a new stop right under the building. By 1989 the Kennedys had landed several government agencies as long-term renters. In an apparent effort to avoid the "appearance of a conflict of interest," Senator Kennedy sold his stake in the property to his dad's trust company, Joseph P. Kennedy Enterprises. Today the Small Business Administration and other federal agencies have multimillion-dollar lease contracts there. The building is valued in excess of $200 million.[6]

Matching the family's zeal for economic and racial justice is their posturing as defenders of the environment. Ted Kennedy not only boasts a near perfect voting record with the League of Conservation Voters; nearly every president over the past thirty years has had to suffer his attacks and ridicule of their environmental record. In recent years he has been joined in this cause by his nephew Joe Kennedy II, who served in Congress for several years, and by his son Patrick, a congressman from Rhode Island. Robert F. Kennedy Jr. heads up an environmental group called the Riverkeeper Alliance and wrote a scathing book attacking the environmental commitment of George W. Bush.

All of the Kennedys have been longtime cheerleaders for alternative sources of energy. Senator Kennedy has introduced dozens of pieces of legislation over the years to encourage the development of solar, hydrogen, and wind as alternatives to oil and coal. As far back as 1980, when he ran for president, he was calling for a greater use of alternative energy to become a central part of our energy policy. He was a cosponsor of the 2005 Clean Power Act, which would require a reduction in power plant emissions, which he said "cause deaths and contribute to global warming." Joe and Patrick have backed the same sort of legislation in the House. Robert Kennedy has crisscrossed the country, decrying our "addiction" to oil and calling for a new era of "clean energy."

During a recent speech to the National Press Club, Senator Kennedy said that we need to "start demanding immediate action to reduce global warming and prevent catastrophic climate change that may be on our horizon now." Part of the answer was to shift to alternative sources: "We should replace our dependence on foreign oil, not by drilling in the priceless Arctic National Wildlife Refuge in Alaska, but by investing in clean energy."

When the Kennedys are not peddling pro-environmental legislation, they are preaching greater environmental consciousness to others as an ethical imperative, telling people that what they do individually can make a difference. On Earth Day 1992, for example, Senator Kennedy went to the University of Massachusetts and told assembled students (and children visiting from nearby schools) the following story.

"An old man walking along the beach at dawn saw a young man picking up starfish and throwing them into the sea. The young man explained that the starfish were stranded on the beach and would die in the morning sun. 'But the beach goes on for miles,' the old man said, 'and there are so many starfish. How can your efforts make any difference?' The young man looked at the starfish in his hand and then threw it safely in the sea. 'It makes a difference to this one.' "[7]

All of this must have been very encouraging to Jim Gordon when he decided to develop and build a "clean energy" project in Massachusetts. With their commitment to clean energy, the search for alternatives to coal and oil, and an ethic that says individuals can make a difference, Gordon must have assumed that the Kennedys would support him. But he soon discovered that the Kennedys have "clean energy" in mind for other people—not themselves.

In 2003, after several years of research and study, Gordon and his fellow investors launched the Cape Wind Project in an effort to provide clean energy for thousands of homes on Cape Cod. Their hope was to replace the coal-fired plants that were providing much of the area's power and were believed to be causing health problems. The Cape Wind Project was expected to provide three-quarters of the electrical power needed by the Cape and other islands without producing pollution or greenhouse gases. This was not a radical or untried plan. Both Sweden and Denmark (two countries that Kennedy often praises as paragons of enlightened social policy) use similar wind-power systems near their coasts.

But from the moment the Kennedy family got wind of these plans (so to speak), they came out in strong opposition. Their complaint: The wind turbines would be built in Nantucket Sound, about six miles off the coast from the Kennedy compound in Hyannis. The problem was not aesthetic; the Kennedys wouldn't be able to actually see the turbines from their home. Instead Robert Kennedy Jr., who had been beating the drum for alternative sources of energy for more than a decade, complained that the project would be built in one of the family's favorite sailing and yachting areas. The Kennedys were quickly joined by other affluent environmentalists with homes in the area, including newscaster Walter Cronkite and historian David McCullough, and the media war began.

When the U.S. Army Corps of Engineers was assigned to conduct a comprehensive review of the proposal, Cape Wind was optimistic that the results would sway the plan's opponents. "I believe that when he [Kennedy] sees the results of this comprehensive environmental review, he will see the compelling public interest benefits: lower electrical costs, a cleaner, healthy environment, and energy independence and minimal environmental impact," said Gordon.

Cronkite, sensitive to criticism that he was being hypocritical, changed his position to "neutral." Senator

Kennedy made a judicious pronouncement to the effect that the idea needed further study. "We have an obligation to preserve it [the Cape] for future generations, which requires us to know the impact of our decisions on the landscape, seascape, and environment," he said publicly. Privately, he tried to get the study canceled.[8]

In early November 2004, shortly after the presidential elections, the U.S. Army Corps of Engineers released a massive thirty-eight-hundred-page study that looked at every aspect of the project, from its economic feasibility to whether birds would be killed by the giant turbines. The study concluded that the environmental effects would be minimal and that the project would provide "compelling environmental and economic benefits" to the area.

Environmentalist groups immediately lined up behind the project. Greenpeace USA said: "Offshore wind offers an immediate, clean, safe and effective answer to both global warming and energy security." Antinuclear activist Helen Caldecott wrote to Kennedy personally in an attempt to persuade him to embrace the project. But Kennedy wouldn't budge. Days after the report was issued, Kennedy called for greater federal regulation of wind farms and got his longtime friend Sen. John Warner (R-VA), chairman of the Armed Services Committee, to offer an amendment to the defense budget to stop the project. The amendment was presented quickly as a major defense appropriation was being voted on. But some members did take notice and the amendment was withdrawn.[9] As of this writing, Kennedy remains completely opposed to the "clean energy" Cape Wind project.

But the Kennedys' hypocrisy on the environment does not end there. Not only have they tried to prevent alternative sources of energy from being developed when it conflicts with their personal interests; they have themselves profited enormously over the years—and continue to profit today—from their lucrative stake in an industry they profess to hate: oil.

Many people are surprised to learn that the Kennedys have been major players in the oil business and continue to receive sizable checks for crude being pumped from their numerous properties. In part this is because they have actively tried to shroud their involvement from public view. But it is also due to the fact that the liberal public interest groups that monitor the oil industry have avoided bringing attention to them. A few years ago, for example, when Ralph Nader's Public Citizen wrote a book called *Who Owns Congress,* they made a big deal of the fact that three senators (Harry Byrd of Virginia, Bill Roth of Delaware, and Malcolm Wallop of Wyoming) all owned a few shares in some oil companies. The book never mentioned that the Kennedys own two oil companies that were drilling for oil in four American states.

The Kennedys' entry into the oil business began in 1950 when Joe Kennedy bought Arctic Oil, a company that was drilling primarily in Texas and Oklahoma. He subsequently bought two oil companies, Kenoil, incorporated in Delaware in 1961, and Mokeen Oil Company four days later.

The family made several million when the Kennedy oil companies struck a large deposit in the McAllen Field in Hidalgo County, Texas, and had another successful well in Louisiana. But they also acquired mineral rights to hundreds of properties throughout the South, in Texas, Oklahoma, Alabama, Florida, and Mississippi. As was often the case, the landowners who sold them these rights were often poor farmers and rural folk who didn't know what "mineral rights" were. The Kennedys bought these rights for pennies on the dollar and acquired the right to drill on the land forever. Even if the owner sold the land to someone else, the Kennedys' right to drill for crude remained. A look at Kennedy mineral rights holdings through real estate records in Mississippi and Texas reveals that many of these tracts are in the poorest parts of these states, like Jackson County, Texas, and the flatlands of Mississippi. Due to the way these contracts are written, even if oil deposits are found, most of these landowners will see little of the money. In at least one case we know of, Kenoil was sued by an elderly couple in Mississippi who claimed that they were not adequately compensated per the contract they had signed.[10]

Over the course of decades, these oil deposits have generated tens of millions in profits for the Kennedy clan. Even today, according to financial disclosures, extended family members each get approximately $50,000 to $100,000 a year from these properties. In total, family revenue from crude oil and natural gas is more than $1 million a year.

Sounding a favorite family theme, Robert Kennedy Jr. has repeatedly said, "The best measure of democracy is how we distribute the goods of the earth." In a 1999 interview with Canada's National Post, he explained that this was particularly true when it comes to natural resources like oil. "Environmental advocacy addresses the question of how you allocate society's wealth, society's natural resources, the bounties of the land, and whether they're being allocated fairly among all of the people." Like every other member of the Kennedy clan, Robert Kennedy Jr. receives his cut of the family's oil and gas royalties. Will he return the money? Better yet, will he ask his family to grant back the exclusive oil rights they have enjoyed for over half a century in the name of social justice?

In the 1970s, fed up with what he called "excessive profits by oil companies," Ted Kennedy led a battle in the Senate to cut the tax loopholes that the industry enjoyed. Capitalizing on the oil shock of the late 1970s, which had sent oil and gas prices soaring during the Carter years, he made the greed of the oil industry a central pillar of his campaign against Carter in 1980 when he challenged him for the Democratic nomination. He claimed that Carter was out to "boost the already ample profits of the oil industry, put millions of consumers through the wringer, and sharpen the class division in our society." His nephew Joseph P. Kennedy II, who was getting ready to run for office, echoed the charge, complaining that the oil industry was "picking our bones clean." (For the record, Joe gets his check from oil royalties, too.)

To punish the industry for its "greed" and cut back on these "excessive profits," Kennedy led a drive to kill the 22 percent depletion allowance for oil companies, claiming that the tax breaks amounted to "welfare." But when Kennedy wrote the legislation, he drew a very interesting distinction between what he called "small struggling oil producers" and the "already cash-rich companies." While large companies lost their loopholes, smaller producers kept their tax shelters. Guess which side of the tax wall the Kennedy holdings fell into?

Since he wrote that bill, the Kennedys have taken depletion allowances and intangible drilling deductions (i.e., "welfare") worth hundreds of thousands of dollars.[11] What's more, they have figured out a way to largely avoid paying corporate taxes on their oil profits altogether. Because Kenoil and Mokeen were oil companies, they needed to pay corporate taxes. So in 1985 the family came up with an ingenious idea: convert their corporate oil holdings to a so-called "royalty trust."

According to state records, the Kennedys established the Arctic Royalty Limited Partnership in Kansas, Texas, Mississippi, and Delaware. Why switch their oil properties from corporate ownership to a royalty limited partnership? Primarily because corporations pay corporate taxes and royalty trusts do not. So when the Kennedy oil properties earn money today, it gets passed to the Kennedys without any corporate taxes being taken out. In fact, with a royalty trust, you don't even have to pay income taxes. Instead, they just pay the capital gains tax of 15 percent.[12]

Another favorite Kennedy cause is gun control. Over the course of the past thirty years, no one has been more vocal or extreme in his opposition to guns than Ted Kennedy. He has called for an outright ban on handguns, the outlawing of most forms of ammunition, and ending the sale of every rifle except those that could be used for hunting. He has complained that existing gun laws are not enforced and penalties for gun violations need to be increased.

The Kennedy position is straightforward and simple:

Guns don't make people safer. People might be tempted to believe that they do, Kennedy has said, but that is an illusion. Guns are a security problem, not a solution.

So imagine my surprise when I discovered an incident involving Kennedy bodyguard Chuck Stein. In 1986, Stein was arrested at the Russell Senate Office Building in the U.S. Capitol for carrying an unregistered weapon, or should I say weapons. Stein was not carrying a simple peashooter like a .38 or even a .45. Stein was caught with a handgun, *two submachine guns and 146 rounds of ammunition*. Why such a large arsenal? "The senator's primary concern was leaving the city with adequate protection," explained Bob Mann, his spokesman.[13]

Kennedy, always a stickler to see that gun laws are enforced in other cases, tried to get the charges dropped. But the Capitol police remained firm. Later Chuck Stein did get out of legal trouble—thanks to the efforts of two lawyers affiliated with the National Rifle Association.

Few politicians have been as adept as Ted Kennedy at using moral condemnation as a political weapon. The image is compelling: Wealthy patrician fights for the little guy and wants the rich to pay more taxes. Yet for decades, it appears, the Kennedys have done the exact opposite of what they preached when it comes to their personal interests. By obstructing efforts to develop clean energy and profiting from the oil industry, they have demonstrated that their liberalism only goes as far as their front doorstep. Kennedy once lectured a political opponent: "You have to pay more than lip service to the environment."[14] It takes a rare kind of political skill to say that with a straight face.

▶▶ *HILLARY CLINTON*

Greedy Speculator, Corporate Shill, and Petty Tax Avoider

In recent years, no one has more loudly proclaimed their sense of political virtue than Bill and Hillary Clinton. In the words of columnist Charles Krauthammer, they have made a "public fetish" of their virtue. It started back in 1969, when Hillary—now a powerful New York senator increasingly spoken of as a possible future president—took to the podium at Wellesley College to deliver the student commencement address. After attacking Edward Brooke, the black Republican Massachusetts senator who was sitting nearby, she explained that for her generation of women, "our prevailing, acquisitive, and competitive corporate life, including tragically the universities, is not the way of life for us. We're searching for more immediate, ecstatic, and penetrating mode[s] of living." Years later as first lady, when she reread the speech, she remarked that she was struck by how idealistic it was and by how much she still agreed with it. In 1993 she told students on a college campus that they hear "too much about individual gain, about the ethos of selfishness." She, on the other hand, understood the importance of what it means "to be a member of a community." After all, she said, "I want to be idealistic, I want to care about the world. . . . I hope you do as well."[1]

In 1993, Hillary told a reporter that her sense of virtue came from growing up with the idea that you had "an obligation to care for other people, to help them. It wasn't something you did as an afterthought. It was how you lived." In contrast to other public figures, Hillary said that both she and her husband really do live that way. "I have a burning desire to do what I can. A desire to make the world around me—kind of going out in concentric circles—better for everybody." She talked about "being connected to a higher purpose" and the sense of "social mission" that she developed when she was a girl and as an activist at Wellesley.[2] For inspiration she reads the Bible, including "the whole book of James, because I, being a Methodist, am big on deeds as well as words."[3]

For his part, Bill Clinton told New Age guru Marianne Williamson in 1995, somewhat plaintively: "I have a good heart. I really do."

If the Clintons embody the height of political virtue, their opponents symbolize the "dark side" of American politics. Instead of simply stating that they are wrong, the Clintons seem to find them morally evil. The main problem with Republicans, according to the Clintons, is "greed." Conservatives "have an ethic of get it while you can and the heck with everybody else." The Clintons, in contrast, were the voice of "the hardworking Americans . . . who pay the taxes and play by the rules." In their black-and-white world of good and evil, the conservative enemy wanted "a gilded age of greed and selfishness, of irresponsibility and excess," while the Clintons professed to be more "sensitive" to "equality and justice, to the poor and the dispossessed." Bill Clinton warned of the "Republican way: every man for himself, and get it while you can." Hillary (as always, going farther than her husband) proclaimed that the problem was capitalism itself: "We have our economy—the market economy—which knows the price of everything but the value of nothing."[4]

Needless to say, the Clintons themselves would never succumb to these temptations. After all, if you are going to denounce other people for being selfish and greedy, you have got to be on a morally higher plane. As Bill Clinton explained before he was elected president in 1992, he and Hillary were just "middle-class folks" trying to do the right thing. "We're not about money," Hillary said.[5]

But the Clintons have always been about money, and the selfless liberalism that they promote and encourage others to embrace has nothing to do with how they live their own lives. Bill Clinton's boundless appetites for power, food, and sex are well documented. Less well known, but just as ravenous, is Hillary's appetite for the material things of life.

The Clintons have always described themselves as "middle-class folks," far from wealthy. During his first presidential campaign, Clinton repeated ad nauseam that he was "the lowest paid governor in America" and that

Hillary gave up huge amounts of professional income as a lawyer to devote her time to charity. But this was pure mythology. The first year he was governor, the Clintons made $408,000 in 2003 dollars, which put them in the top 1 percent of American wage-earners. In addition, they enjoyed a food allowance of $50,000 per year, free residence in the governor's mansion, an entertainment budget, a state credit card for travel, free babysitting, health insurance, chauffeurs, bodyguards, and so on.

Over the years, Hillary became highly adept at manipulating public office to supplement their income. In the final days of 2000, just as she and her husband were getting ready to leave the White House and before she took her Senate seat, she put out word that she wanted some things for their two new homes. She registered at luxury retailers and calls were made by her friends. "Would you please buy this silverware, these gifts, for Mrs. Clinton for her new house?" they would say. All the gifts needed to be in before January 3, they explained, when Senate ethics rules kicked in.[6]

What she got was a cascade of gifts, including more than $50,000 in flatware, a $3,000 television, a $22,000 glass sculpture, and a $38,000 Dale Chihuly basket set. They even received $9,683 in gifts from Walter Kaye, who had introduced Monica Lewinsky to the White House. In all, they received more than $190,000 in gifts—the bulk of it for Hillary.

Not content with this, however, Hillary and Bill also took with them $360,000 in other gifts that had been donated to the White House. More than $173,000 in art objects and books, $69,000 in furniture, $26,000 in golf equipment, and $24,000 in clothes that were meant for the White House ended up in the Clintons' home in Chappaqua. The White House curator said the shipments occurred on Hillary's orders, though when the scandal went public, Hillary blamed it on a clerical error. But there is no question that Hillary knew they were meant for the White House: None of the items had been claimed on the Clintons' annual tax returns, indicating that they knew they were not the intended recipients.[7]

Even without these supplements, however, the Clintons have since 1979 consistently been among the wealthiest income earners in the country, the group that they (along with other leading Democrats) have repeatedly claimed don't pay their "fair share" in taxes. In the summer of 2004, Hillary told an audience of wealthy contributors: "Many of you are well enough off that . . . the tax cuts may have helped you. We're saying that for America to get back on track, we're probably going to cut that short and not give it to you. *We're going to take things away from you on behalf of the common good.*"

Like the tax-and-spend Democrats they are, the Clintons have always advocated redistributive taxation. What's more, Hillary typically casts the question of taxes in moral terms. "Every decision we make about taxes is a decision about our values," she says. Thus when citizens vote to reduce taxes, the Clintons condemn them. When voters in Virginia rolled back personal property taxes on their cars and trucks in 1997, for instance, Bill Clinton called them "selfish."[8] (This was a particularly ironic charge, since when he was governor of Arkansas, the Clintons failed to pay the personal property tax on Hillary's sporty Fiat.

Only after they were found out did they pay the tax. The governor blamed the snafu on his office staff, inadvertently revealing that he was using state employees for his personal business.)

The Clintons profess not to understand why people don't like to pay their taxes. As Bill Clinton explained recently in a speech before Jesse Jackson's Rainbow Coalition (which has also had its share of tax problems), he and Hillary just *love* paying taxes: "I must be the only person in America that every time—I pay the maximum tax rates—every time I sign that tax form, I smile." Indeed, he said, the IRS should go farther and audit him regularly. "I think they ought to audit me and everyone in my income group every year, because if I make a mistake, I actually think they can make some real money out of me, and I want to pay what I owe."

Yet far from paying the maximum tax bill every time, as Clinton claimed, the Clintons have almost never paid their "fair share." A study of their income tax returns reveals that, since 1991, the Clintons have paid on average about 7 percent *less* to the IRS than others in their income group. While most Americans in their bracket were paying 27 percent in taxes, the Clintons were bumping along at 20 percent.

How did they manage this? In the 1980s the Clintons claimed hundreds of thousands of dollars in write-offs, and they did it without having a large home mortgage to deduct. Instead, in what can only be described as a monument to personal pettiness, they took hugely inflated deductions on personal items donated to charity. They wrote off $30 for a used shower curtain, $40 for an old pair of Bill's running shoes, $5 for a used electric razor, $80 for an old pair of dress shoes, and close to $4 a pair for Bill's used underwear (as if anyone else would want to wear that). When *Money* magazine asked accountants to take a look at their returns, the verdict came back: "The Clintons appear to have repeatedly overstated their charitable contributions."[9]

The Clintons have also claimed thousands in write-offs over the years that they were not entitled to. Most famously, they took numerous deductions on a real estate investment (Whitewater) into which they never actually put any money. When their personal accountant objected, the Clintons brushed him aside. In sworn testimony, Gaines Norton said he told Bill Clinton that the deductions were probably illegal. Clinton told him to "back off and leave the issue alone." A Senate committee investigating Whitewater also disclosed that in 1984–85 the Clintons took thousands in deductions that Hillary admitted at the time she knew they were not entitled to.[10]

On their 1980 return, the Clintons failed to report Hillary's profits from commodities trading (close to $100,000), but instead claimed a loss. They also never reported $74,234 in loans, payments, and forgiven debts that the IRS code counts as income. Had they done so, it would have cost them $13,000 in additional taxes.

Shortly after being elected president in November 1992, Clinton and his advisers sat down to lay out a legislative agenda. Near the top was a plan to increase taxes by creating a "millionaires" rate that would raise the top tax rate from 31 to 36 percent. They planned to make the increase retroactive, meaning that even if Congress passed the bill in the fall of 1993, it would apply to all income earned since January. Meanwhile, as 1992 was coming to an end, Hillary made sure to draw her partnership proceeds in the Rose Law Firm early. In the past, according to their tax returns, she had received these annual payments in January. This time she got $203,172 on December 31, thereby avoiding the retroactive tax increase that was about to take effect.[11]

The Clintons have also been outspoken in their support for the inheritance tax. In 2000, Clinton vetoed a bill seeking to end it, and as senator, Hillary has proclaimed that getting rid of the tax is wrong because it will let the affluent off the hook.[12] But that doesn't necessarily mean that *they* want to pay it. Indeed, the Clintons have set up a contract trust, which among other things allows them to substantially reduce the amount of inheritance tax their estate will have to pay when they die.

The Clintons believe in using the tax code to transfer wealth from the rich to the poor; it's just that they don't have their own wealth in mind.

The Clintons achieved considerable wealth in their early years because of Hillary's work as a lawyer. In Hillary's mind, this was simply a testament to her acumen and skill. She held herself out as a feminist icon of sorts, retaining her maiden name as a sign of independence. (She took Bill's name only when the practice began hurting him politically.) She told the media that she has tried to have "an independent life," that she has had her "own career," and as a feminist was simply seeking a level playing field in the legal profession. Later she offended many American housewives when she said that she "could have stayed home and baked cookies and had teas, but what I decided to do was fulfill my profession."[13]

In her memoirs she writes as if her career was completely detached from her husband's, and that her professional success was simply a function of her feminism. "While Bill talked about social change," she writes of herself in glowing terms, "I embodied it. I had my own opinions, interests and profession."[14]

There is no doubt that Hillary Clinton is smart and shrewd. But she was very far from the independent professional she claimed to be. As feminist writer Karen Lehrman put it, Hillary's rise to prominence came not through her own unaided efforts but by "riding on [her husband's] coattails."[15] Her own career, both as a lawyer and politician, utterly belies her insistence on being viewed as an icon of feminist autonomy.

Hillary was brought on as a lawyer at the prestigious Rose Law Firm in Little Rock two weeks after her husband was elected state attorney general. Two years later, when her husband became governor, she made partner. She did very little litigation at the firm and instead was a rainmaker, with responsibility for bringing in new clients. Given her husband's political prominence, she was well positioned to do so. Utility companies, manufacturing firms, investment brokers, you name it: Anyone with business before the state was interested in retaining the governor's wife. The Little Rock Airport Commission asked her to represent them and paid her $360,000 over the years, though there is no evidence that she had any particular expertise in this area. Her legal income soared from $50,000 to $200,000 overnight.

At the same time, Clinton regularly appointed his wife to positions that she was, by any objective standard, not highly qualified to hold. When he put her in charge of a fifteen-member state committee on school reform, one reporter questioned her qualifications. "I've gone to school a large part of my life," she said, "and I've been involved in classroom activities and visiting with teachers as a volunteer." The same could have been said by many housewives in the state. Later, when Clinton was elected president, she was appointed head of a commission to reform the $850 billion health care industry even though she had no experience in the field, save for a stint on an Arkansas health care commission.[16]

Hillary's ride on her husband's coattails also led her into the corporate world in a very real and direct way.

Corporations have always figured in the Clinton lexicon as purveyors of a particular kind of evil. In the 1992 presidential campaign, Bill Clinton compared the typical American CEO to "a street corner crack dealer."[17] Over the course of his public life, Bill and Hillary have affixed the word "greed" to pharmaceutical companies, oil companies, chemical companies, power companies, and of course, Republicans and conservatives. Other corporate crimes include "price-gouging," "cost-shifting," and general "profiteering." They complain about "self-serving CEOs try[ing] to build an economy out of paper and perks."[18]

In 1979, Hillary wrote an article calling for a legal crusade against corporate America. Published as a chapter in a book called *Children's Rights: Contemporary Perspectives,* it called for lawsuits against the nuclear power industry, manufacturers of "junk food," and other corporations that have a "negative effect" on young people. Among the corporate malefactors she targeted were the television and automobile industries, pharmaceutical companies, and others that abuse the "extraordinary power they hold over all of us, but particularly over our children" to extract illicit profits. A few years later, in a speech to high school students at the so-called Governor's School in Arkansas, she explained that it wasn't big government that scared her, but big business.

Yet as a partner in the Rose Law Firm, Hillary made a great deal of money representing a wide range of corporate interests. And the advice she gave them often involved showing companies ways to avoid government regulation. When some friends of the Clintons purchased the Castle Sewer and Water Company as part of their plan to develop a residential area called Castle Grande, they hired Hillary to answer a very direct question about environmental regulations. Should they register their sewer system as a public utility with the Arkansas Public Service Commission (PSC)? Hillary and her associate Rick Donovan advised them not to, since as a public utility they would be regulated by the PSC. Instead, she advised them simply to take their chances. If an environmental problem was reported by a resident, it would become a legal matter they could fight in court, and in the worst case it would mean paying a fine. That would be better than facing constant regulation by the state.

With her husband's political rise, Hillary was soon to be found on numerous corporate boards. She earned $31,000 a year sitting on the board of the Lafarge Corporation, an American subsidiary of a French company that was the second-largest producer of cement in the United States. Lafarge in turn owned a company that burned hazardous waste in cement kilns, much to the chagrin of residents in Ohio, California, Arizona, and Texas.[19] When the parent company was caught in a price-fixing scandal in 1991, Hillary Clinton said nothing. When it fought bitterly with a striking union at one of its cement plants, she toed the corporate line.[20] While sitting on the board of TCBY Yogurt, she defended the firm against shareholder lawsuits claiming that executives were being given "golden parachutes."[21] She sat on the board of Wal-Mart and seemed content with everything the company was doing, even though it was under fire from labor unions, feminists, and civil rights groups on charges of union-busting, sexism, and racism in their hiring practices.

Even Hillary's "charitable causes" could be quite profitable. The Clintons touted her work for the Southern Development Corporation, an organization put together by local charities to give loans to businesses in poor rural areas. Hillary sat on the board of directors, where she received no compensation. But she did solicit and receive a retainer for her legal services from the charity. Over the course of her five-year tenure, the corporation would make $1 million in loans to poor people—and pay Rose Law Firm some $150,000 in legal fees.[22]

The Clintons may not be "about money," but that's no reason not to seek the maximum return on your investments. Thus, even as Hillary spoke out against the dangers of big business and the gilded age of excess in

Reagan's America, she was obsessed with her own stock portfolio. Her broker, Roy Drew of E. F. Hutton in Little Rock, recalls: "I recommended Diamond Shamrock and a movie deal and Firestone. And Hillary would call and say, 'What's Firestone doing?' And I'd say, 'Well, it's up an eighth today,' and she'd say, 'Why isn't it doing anything?' She was used to the fast action of cattle futures. The next day she'd call and say, 'Where's Firestone?' And I'd say, 'Down a half,' and she'd say, 'Oh, no, what's the matter?' She'd call three or four times a week."[23]

In another interview he explained, "She was doing the same thing as all those yuppies who she said represented the decade of greed. . . . Money was extremely important to the Clintons."[24]

According to the *New Yorker*, in 1979, Hillary and a friend attended a party in Little Rock, where she started making "rather pious pronouncements" about the commodities market. "They saw it as too laissez-faire," one guest recalled. "They were leaning toward more government regulation, rules." Hillary told the group that she disdained the whole principle of making money through commodities speculation and condemned it as "not socially acceptable, dealing in such large sums of money, such greed." Of course, she herself stayed in the market and kept all of her profits.

Friends of Hillary's like Marian Wright Edelman were involved in the anti-apartheid movement and supported bringing sanctions against South Africa. But that didn't stop Hillary from buying one hundred shares of stock in De Beers, the South African diamond consortium. (She took a capital gain on that stock in 1981.) For good measure, she also bought shares in Engelhard, the South African mining company. (When Clinton lost the governorship in 1980, he went to work for a firm called Intermark, which also did considerable business in South Africa.)

Hillary had attacked chemical and oil companies as being threats to the environment. But shortly after writing those words, she herself went into the oil business, investing in an oil-drilling partnership based in Colorado. In addition to pumping crude, she also received a handy tax deduction.[25]

When they entered the White House, Hillary remained in a private investment partnership called Value Partners and refused to place it in a blind trust. Every president since Nixon had set up a blind trust to avoid having a conflict of interest, but Hillary didn't believe it was necessary, apparently because she was beyond reproach. Shortly before she officially launched her health care reform program, the investment fund shorted millions of dollars of the portfolio in pharmaceutical stocks, betting that their value would plunge. The fund also took a stake in United Healthcare, an HMO that stood to benefit under the Clinton plan.

Then consider the Whitewater investment. Forget for a minute about all the scandal associated with the word and the convoluted financing arrangements. Look at it for a minute as a pure investment—the biggest business venture that the Clintons had ever been involved in prior to the presidency.

Back in 1978, Bill Clinton was a popular Arkansas attorney general running for governor. He was campaigning as a reformer, an advocate of "consumer protection" and "rights for the elderly." Like Hillary, he was concerned about unscrupulous "private corporations." And as he has so often done in his public career, he made a point of claiming the moral high ground over his opponent.[26]

An old friend and political operative, Jim McDougall, came to Bill and Hillary with an investment idea. He wanted to purchase 230 acres of land situated along the White River in the Ozark Mountains of north Arkansas and subdivide it to sell lots as vacation sites. McDougall promised huge returns, on the order of 20 percent a year. The Clintons thought it sounded like a great plan. Hillary in particular had high hopes for the property. While publicly criticizing Ronald Reagan's tax cuts, she wrote McDougall in 1981: "If Reaganomics works at all, Whitewater could become the western hemisphere's Mecca."[27]

The Clintons put no money into the investment. But Hillary, as an attorney in private practice, played an important role in establishing and running the venture. And what a venture it was meant to be. Whitewater was not designed as a regular real estate company. The plan was to sell lots, mainly to elderly retirees and middle-class families, by advertising in small-town newspapers. (They advertised several times in *Mother Earth News*.) Ordinarily, of course, when you buy a piece of land and finance the purchase, you receive a copy of the deed. If you start missing payments and can't work things out with the finance company, they will eventually repossess the property. After paying off fees and debts, you will get back any remaining equity.

But the Clintons and McDougall did things differently. When customers wanted to buy a lot, they signed a simple purchase agreement. But this was no ordinary real estate contract. The small print at the bottom read: "In the event the default continues for 30 days . . . payments made by the purchaser *shall be considered as rent* for the use of the premises." In other words, the buyers did not actually take ownership of their property until the final payment was made. If a buyer missed just one monthly payment, all their previous payments would be classified as rent and they would have no equity in the land at all.

This sort of contract was illegal in many other states, because it was considered exploitative of the poor and uneducated.[28] One look at the experience of those who bought into Whitewater and you can see why.

Clyde Soapes was a grain-elevator operator from Texas who heard about the lots in early 1980 and jumped at the chance to invest. He put $3,000 down and began making payments of $244.69 per month. He made *thirty-five* payments in all—totaling $11,564.15, just short of the $14,000 price for the lot. Then he suddenly fell ill with diabetes and missed a payment, then two. The Clintons informed him that he had lost the land and all of his money. There was no court proceeding or compensation. Months later they resold his property to a couple from Nevada for $16,500. After they too missed a payment, the Clintons resold it yet again.

Soapes and the couple from Nevada were not alone. *More than half* of the people who bought lots in Whitewater—teachers, farmers, laborers, and retirees—made payments, missed one or two, and then lost their land without getting a dime of their equity back. According to Whitewater records, at least sixteen different buyers paid more than $50,000 and never received a property deed. The Clintons continued this approach up until the 1992 election, when they tried to quietly get out of the investment.[29]

I say "the Clintons" did these things because Hillary was at the center of it all. Monthly payment checks were sent to the Whitewater Development Corporation in care of Hillary Rodham Clinton. In 1982, Hillary herself sold a home to Hillman Logan, who went bankrupt and then died. She took possession of the home and resold it to another buyer for $20,000. No one was compensated (and she didn't report the sale on her tax return).

Hillary has always very indignantly maintained that she and her husband "did nothing wrong" with regard to Whitewater. After all, they lost money in the deal. But they have always avoided discussions about how the business was structured, and how it exploited the very people they have often professed to help. In the meantime, Sen. Hillary Clinton has gone on to champion the cause of going after banks and other lenders for "predatory mortgage lending practices." In an amazing feat of moral dexterity, she cosponsored the Predatory Consumer Lending Act, claiming that mortgage fees are too high. (No, the law does not outlaw the type of financing scheme she was involved in.)[30]

Then there is her long-standing public concern about child welfare. Ever since her days at Yale Law School, Hillary Clinton has been a staunch advocate of children's rights. Believing that parents are often too authoritarian, she has fought for children's rights for more than thirty years. In her first article, published by the *Harvard Education Review* in 1973 and titled "Children Under the Law," she referred to children as "child citizens" and advocated reversing the judicial presumption that children are incompetent before the law. Society should treat children as mini-adults unless they can be shown to be incompetent. In other words, children are competent to make the major decisions in their own lives unless proven otherwise.

In 1977, Hillary expanded on this view in an essay for the book *Children's Rights: Contemporary Perspectives.* In addition to arguing that we should sue major corporations to protect children, she maintained that children were competent to make "decisions about motherhood and abortion, schooling, cosmetic surgery, treatment of venereal disease, or employment and others . . . Children should have the right to be permitted to decide their own future if they are competent."

A guiding light in Hillary's thinking on this issue was the dissenting opinion of the Supreme Court in *Wisconsin v Yoder* (1912). The Court allowed three Amish families to keep their children out of high school even though there was a state law requiring attendance. Justice William O. Douglas, dissenting, noted that no one had asked the children what they wanted to do. "These children are entitled to be heard," he wrote. They should be "masters of their own destiny." Hillary was obviously enamored of that opinion, because she cited it several times in articles and speeches.

Hillary has gone so far as to compare the struggle for children's rights with the civil rights movement and equal rights for women. In her view, children are arbitrarily excluded from full citizenship because of a form of bigotry. As the late Christopher Lasch put it in 1992, Hillary is "opposed to the principle of parental authority in any form."[31]

The subject of children's rights became a hot topic during the 1992 presidential campaign. Hillary was eager to avoid the issue, but Clinton loyalist Garry Wills defended her controversial views. "In the past, the child's rights were asserted vicariously through the parent," he wrote. "Mrs. Clinton sees those rights as, at times, to be asserted against the parent." When Wills asked her during the campaign whether her views on children's rights had changed over the years, she assured him that they had not.[32]

To make her point, young Chelsea was trotted out as proof that the Clintons, too, were practicing what was called "children's rights on a small scale." It was Chelsea, they told the media, who had been given the choice of where she wanted to go to church. She picked Hillary's Methodist faith over her father's Baptist congregation.[33]

Today, Hillary openly opposes calls for "parental notification" in the event that a teenager wants an abortion. In practical terms, this means that she believes pregnant thirteen- and fourteen-year-old girls are generally competent to make this momentous decision without their parents' consent or involvement.[34]

Yet when it came to her own daughter, Hillary showed a very different, much more authoritarian side of her parental personality. When Chelsea, at thirteen, wanted to get her ears pierced, Hillary wouldn't let her. Hillary detested ear piercing (she wore clip-ons) and local ordinances in the nation's capital—thank goodness!—required that adolescent girls get parental approval for a piercing. She also denied Chelsea's right to wear makeup. Children's rights might be a "logical extension" of the civil rights movement—but that doesn't give you the right to wear just anything. "You're wearing that?" she would frequently ask, sending Chelsea back to her room to get something else for school.[35] The poor girl couldn't even set her own bedtime. While living at home the teenager had a strict curfew: 10 P.M. on school nights, 11:30 on weekends. "She has a fault that her father has," Hillary warned ominously. "She would stay up too late if I let her."[36]

What she watched on television was also strictly controlled. She was allowed to watch shows like *Murphy Brown, Designing Women,* and *Evening Shade,* but that was about it. (No MTV or HBO.) At the movies, it was strictly PG-13. When she turned sixteen, the word came down from on high: "Sixteen gives you a license to stay up a little late, but not on a school night."[37]

Hillary Clinton might see herself as the liberator of America's children, believing that they should become "masters of their own destiny," but her own daughter found her to be "overprotective."[38] How come this kid never got a lawyer?

Hillary has also been a lifelong proponent of public schools and a staunch critic of any effort to make private schools more accessible to the middle class and poor. During the 1992 campaign the Clintons made a point of stating that they, unlike then-president George H. W.

Bush, were "members of the middle class" and repeatedly mentioned, in front of black audiences, that their daughter went to an integrated public school.[39] Putting children in private schools meant "giving up on public education," Hillary said, and during the 1992 campaign the Clintons made frequent visits to public schools as an emblem of their commitment to the system. Bill Clinton visited Jefferson Junior High in Washington, D.C., and praised the school for its national recognition in math and science. Hillary visited Washington's Hine Junior High and in front of the assembly told them what a wonderful job they were doing.[40]

Hillary has always explained her opposition to vouchers by claiming: "There is evidence that they drain dollars and students from the public schools and we need those dollars and students."[41] But apparently they didn't "need" her own daughter. After the 1992 election, when it was time to select a school for Chelsea, D.C. officials expected "a signal of confidence in urban education" from the Clintons. Sen. Ron Wyden of Oregon, whose son Adam attended a public elementary school in Washington, urged them to do the same with Chelsea because "Washington has good public schools."[42] The last Democrat in the White House, Jimmy Carter, had also sent his daughter to a D.C. public school. (Amy Carter attended Stevens, a public elementary school just eight blocks from the White House.)

Instead, the Clintons selected the elite Sidwell Friends school. Apparently they had concluded that public education was a great and glorious thing—for someone else's kids. The announcement came just hours after Hillary paid a visit to Rockefeller Elementary, a public school in Little Rock where the students had put together a collage of photographs from the presidential campaign. Hillary once again spoke movingly about the importance of public education and her concerns about sustaining it.

Ironically, the very schools that the Clintons rejected for Chelsea were the ones they had so lavishly praised a few months earlier. Living in the White House, she could have attended either Jefferson or Hine. Jefferson was particularly strong in what, according to her parents, interested Chelsea most—science and math. "The important point was to make the right choice for Chelsea," said White House aide George Stephanopoulos. "We can't put politics in a personal, family decision."[43] Suddenly the Clintons were no longer icons of the "middle class" or defenders of public education. They were parents, making the same kind of private decision that they had criticized others for making. Jimmy Carter, who seemed at least to practice what he preached, professed to be "very disappointed" by their decision, given Amy's fine experience in D.C. public schools.[44]

In the Clintons' moral universe, their own motives and intentions are always pure. Their adversaries, on the other hand, are animated by selfishness and greed, a conservative disease to which they claim to be immune. Through all the contradictions in their lives, and despite their voluminous reflections on themselves, they seem utterly clueless about their own greed and avarice, all the while continuing to offer unsought advice about how other people can live up to their exalted moral standards.

▶▶ *RALPH NADER*

Bourgeois Materialist, Stock Manipulator, and Tyrannical Sweatshop Boss

Noam Chomsky has his million-dollar-plus vacation home and Michael Moore his Manhattan penthouse and north woods log home. Hillary Clinton may spend $4,500 on a cashmere sweater. But Ralph Nader is the spartan of the liberal-left. His frugality is legendary. Living in a rooming house with a public bathroom down the hallway, he owns no car and has kept his material wants to a minimum. He claims to live on just $25,000 a year. He won't eat hot dogs or any other processed food. When he left the army in 1958 after spending eight months as a cook, he bought twelve pairs of shoes and four dozen socks at the PX. He was still wearing them three decades later.[1]

Nader's parents were Lebanese immigrants who settled in Connecticut. The Naders were austere and frugal in the extreme. When Ralph had a birthday, his mother would bake a cake and frost it. But after he blew out the candles, she would remove the frosting before he was allowed to eat the cake. The frosting was for picture-taking, not eating.[2]

"Saint Ralph," he has been called by his followers. On *Hollywood Squares,* Phyllis Diller once called Ralph Nader "the most honest man in America." Comedian Jimmy Tingle declared in 2000 that "Ralph Nader is the most principled public figure in America today." As early as 1976 there were murmurs in the media about how Nader needed to run for president. Nicholas von Hoffman and Mary McGrory both wrote articles begging him to save the republic. Despite this prodding from his fans and friends, Nader didn't make his first run until 1992; but he hasn't missed an election since. In none of the four presidential bids has he ever received much popular support. But he remains an icon of the Left, seemingly untouched by the dirty side of politics and modern consumer society.

Ralph Nader has made a lack of interest in material things one of the defining principles of his life. When it comes to issues like pollution, inequality, corporate power, even automobile safety, he sees the source of these great evils as the avarice of corporations and an overconsumptive America. Americans in his mind are too materialistic, too bent on making money. When he visited Soviet Russia in the early 1960s, the shortage of goods and food supplies did not bother him. Indeed, he found the communist-induced poverty liberating, telling one reporter that he "liked the absence of automobiles" and loved the basic food of vegetables and potatoes. "It was still solid, basic food rather than the sleezy processed stuff we get," he said.[3]

When he returned to Moscow shortly after the fall of the Berlin Wall, he was "shocked" to discover that Soviet officials were praising free-market economist Milton Friedman. He denounced plans to privatize Soviet television (claiming that it would give opportunities to corporations) and was surprised by complaints from Russian citizens that they had to stand in line for hours to obtain food and other basic supplies. "Some people say that because the Soviet people have to stand in line, it gives them time to reflect and become philosophical," Nader said to a small group in Moscow. The entire audience laughed at him.[4]

That fanatical obsession with health and safety has always been part of Nader's essence. After pushing for auto safety, energy safety, and food safety, he continues his crusade down some strange alleys. Thus he's opposed to bottled water because it lulls the "contented classes" into apathy over issues like clean water. He launched an ill-fated campaign against "rock 'n' roll deafness" and suggested to two U.S. senators that they pass a law to force members of rock bands to wear ear protectors.

To his friends, that obsessional drive can be a little hard to take. The writer Michael Kinsley used to work with Nader, and like so many others, he left somewhat disillusioned by Nader's fanaticism. "In this world of sinners," he writes, "not everyone wants to live on raw vegetables and set the thermostat at sixty." When one of his friends mentioned that his daughter was keeping a turtle as a pet, Nader called the little girl directly to warn her that turtles "transmit salmonella." He has advised other friends to get rid of their house cats because they supposedly cause leukemia.

In Nader's view, people don't know their own interests. As he told one audience in New Jersey, "As long as this country is populated by people who fritter away their citizenship, fritter it away watching TV or playing cards or mah-jongg, or just generally being slobs, it will never be the country we should want it to be."[5]

Nader made a name for himself back in the 1960s by taking on General Motors. He proclaimed that the Corvair was "unsafe at any speed" and wrote a best-selling book on the subject. Since then he has been the consummate anticorporate crusader. For more than forty years he has warned that we are "falling into corporatist control" and promoting "domination by a pro-corporate oligarchy." The problem is not just individual companies like GM, but the very nature of corporations themselves. Nader fears "the dominant power of large corporations in this country" and has accused corporate leaders of using illegitimate tax breaks and government manipulation to expand their power, establish monopolies, and avoid democratic control. But corporations are not just irresponsible; they threaten our health and well-being. According to Nader, they have "eroded our standards of living—and sometimes living itself."

Instead of buying goods from corporations, he has advocated the establishment of "consumer-owned private enterprises at the community level." Nader suggests that people join together, invest in a co-op, and buy goods from themselves, as it were, rather than from evil corporations. There certainly are numerous co-ops today around the country.[6] Yet Nader himself has invested millions in corporations and comparatively little in his highly touted "co-ops."

Indeed, despite his spartan lifestyle, Ralph Nader is a wealthy man. But little is known about his appetite for corporate investment because he is one of the most secretive political figures in recent American history. This is especially ironic, insofar as one of Nader's most consistent messages has been the need for greater openness in business and politics alike. "Information," he declares, "is the currency of democracy; its denial must always be suspect." Public officials, corporations, and the government need to end secrecy because "knowledge is essential to democracy."[7] He is particularly suspicious of corporate secrecy. "Secrecy often seems the first rule of corporate bureaucracies," he has observed.[8] But it also seems to be the first rule of Ralph Nader, who over the course of three decades has put together a political and activist empire that has diligently worked to shroud from view its resources, connections, and operations.

Nader has famously and publicly over the years stuck to the story that he owns no home but lives his life of activism in a small apartment in northwest Washington, D.C. But his friends and coworkers know better. Back in the 1970s, neighbors in an exclusive Washington neighborhood spotted Nader coming and going from an expensive home, worth approximately $2 million, on Bancroft Place. A check of real estate records reveals that the home was not in Nader's name, but in that of his unemployed brother Shafeek. (His brother claimed that he was an education consultant, but he kept an unlisted number.) Later, ownership was transferred to Nader's sister Claire, who works with him on his various projects. When asked about the house by Maxine Cheshire of the *Washington Post*, Nader admitted that he did indeed use the house for personal reasons. Then he went on to talk about the great tax breaks that came from owning the home. Said Cheshire, "He talks about that real estate investment the way some men talk about sex. He's so excited about the whole idea of tax write-offs and all that. I mean, did I realize that that's the greatest investment you can make, the biggest tax advantage, bla bla bla bla bla bla."

This is a bit surprising, coming from a man who thinks the biggest problem in America is corporate greed and the refusal of the rich to pay their share. "Get the rich off welfare," he has said. "Make them pay their taxes."[9]

When traveling to give speeches around the country, Nader not only commands a nice fee, but also demands numerous perks. As one official with a trial lawyer association told *Forbes* magazine, "Oh, God, limousines and nothing but the best hotels. We got quite a bill when he was in town."[10]

Because Nader's organizations are charities, they are required by law to register in individual states in order to solicit donations. This involves filing an annual report, including a summary of how donations are spent. The practice was established to protect individual donors from being robbed by unscrupulous fund-raisers, and it would seem to be the sort of regulation that Nader would support. But he actually has a terrible record of complying with the requirements. According to a detailed study made in the early 1980s, Nader's organization Public Citizen was in violation of the statute in twenty-three states. They had simply failed repeatedly, over the course of half a dozen years, to file the statements required by law. Nader's National Citizens Committee for Broadcasting had failed to apply or ask for a tax exemption in twenty-five states. A third organization, the Center for the Study of Responsive Law, had failed to register anywhere. When it finally did register in New York, it failed the following year to submit the required annual report and then had its right to solicit in that state revoked.[11]

This pattern of failing to file reports continues. For the first twenty years of the Center for the Study of Responsive Politics' existence, the IRS never received the legally required 990 form from the group. All but one of Nader's eighteen organizations failed to register or obtain licensing from Washington, D.C.'s Department of Consumer Regulatory Affairs.[12]

Nader has likewise been very secretive about his personal finances. He may champion openness and accountability for other public figures, but when he first ran for president in 1992, he refused to release any information about his finances, even though Bush, Clinton, and Ross Perot had done so. When he ran four years later, he again refused to allow Americans to know even the slightest of his financial details. To make sure he could keep the information secret, he made a point in both elections of spending less than five thousand dollars so he wouldn't have to file a financial disclosure form with the Federal Election Commission.

When he ran for a third time, in 2000, there was

mounting pressure on Nader to release financial information. In part the pressure arose because he was likely to influence the election, and his critics on the left wanted him to disclose his financial interests. He finally relented, but he still refused to release his tax returns, though his opponents Al Gore and George W. Bush had already done so.

Over the course of thirty years, Nader has made a career out of blasting corporate America for just about every imaginable crime, in the process earning millions of dollars in speaking fees and royalties. In particular, he has repeatedly railed against stock "speculation" on Wall Street. What has Nader done with all that money? Turned around and invested it—not in those co-ops he's always pushing—but in the very multinational corporations that he so frequently decries as being bad corporate citizens.

Nader may have denounced "rampant speculation on Wall Street," but that hasn't stopped him from selling short or investing in companies that might be influenced by his political activities.[13] Over the years he has proven to be a shrewd investor, picking stocks that have high profit margins, spotty or nonexistent records with organized labor, and a history of compromising involvement in Third World countries. He has publicly attacked other Americans for using a vile "corporate yardstick" to determine whether the economy is successful based on "sales and profits" and has called for one that speaks of enhanced quality of life and advancing the cause of social justice.[14] But he certainly doesn't pick his stocks that way.

In the sixteen months leading up to his 2000 presidential run, Nader gave fifty-nine speeches for which he was paid between $5,000 and $15,000 each. Overall, his paid speeches brought in $300,000 during that period. When pressed to explain just how much money he had made from his activism, Nader was forced to admit that he had probably netted about $14 million over the years in honorariums and book royalties. His personal portfolio included more than $2.1 million in corporate stock, accounting for more than half of his net worth of $3.8 million. He may have crusaded against corporate "criminals," "crooks," and "greed," but that didn't stop him from owning more than $1 million in Cisco Systems. He also owns $250,000 in the mutual fund Fidelity Magellan, which invests in oil companies, defense contractors, and the sort of large multinationals he is always railing against.[15]

When challenged on his investments, Nader gave what can only be called the Noam Chomsky defense. "Do you have money in the bank?" he asked a reporter in Santa Monica. "Do you have a checking account? You're condemned because that bank owns stock. See?"[16] This was the same sort of twisted logic that Chomsky has used to justify taking money from the Pentagon. In some indirect way, he argues, everyone benefits from the Pentagon or the stock market, so there is nothing wrong with his doing so directly. But Nader claims not to invest in just any companies; he follows strict investment principles: "No. 1, they're not monopolists and No. 2, they don't produce land mines, napalm, weapons." But Cisco controls about 89 percent of the router market on the Internet. And as we will see, through a trust he also owns a huge chunk of stock in Verizon, which is also a monopoly in certain regions of the country.

Moreover, not only does he own shares of General Dynamics through his Fidelity mutual fund; he also owns shares in General Electric and IBM, two major defense contractors, through his private trust. They must be profitable investments because he sees these companies as driving the arms race. "I'm quite aware of how the arms race is driven by corporate demands for contracts, whether it's General Dynamics or Lockheed Martin," Nader told the *Progressive* in April 2000. "They drive it through Congress. They drive it by hiring Pentagon officials in the Washington military industrial complex, as Eisenhower phrased it." The Fidelity Magellan fund owns 2,041,800 shares of General Dynamics, as a vigilant investor like Nader could easily verify by a glance at their annual report.

Before the House Budget Committee in June 1999, Nader testified that "Bristol-Myers Squibb markets taxol at a wholesale price that is nearly 20 times its manufacturing cost. A single injection of taxol can cost patients considerably more than $2,000 and treatment requires multiple injections." The Fidelity Magellan fund owns 15,266,900 shares of Bristol-Myers Squibb.[17] There's nothing wrong with that, of course—unless you hold yourself out as a paragon of socially responsible investment and denounce other people for putting money into morally suspect corporate enterprises.

Nader maintains that he has given the bulk of his money—90 percent of it in fact—to the causes he believes in rather than putting it in his own pocket. But that claim is patently false, if for no other reason than that it would be illegal: The IRS allows you to donate a maximum of 50 percent of your earnings to charity. The rest you must pay taxes on. Meanwhile, a look at Nader's private charitable foundations indicates that his donations are way down in recent years.

Nader has two charitable foundations: the Safety Systems Foundation and the Public Safety Research Institute (PSRI). Michael Moore, as we saw earlier, has followed his example. The establishment of these foundations is particularly ironic in Nader's case because he has denounced this very practice as a way of avoiding taxes when other people have done it. In one of his studies, called "The Company State," Nader attacked the Du Pont family for "having avoided the payment of inheritance taxes by leaving the bulk of their estate to a charitable foundation." Nader is using the exact same clause in the tax code for his foundation.

Moreover, despite his claims to have donated the bulk of his earnings to his causes, IRS records show that in 2000, despite earning close to $300,000 in speaking fees alone, he made only one $8,000 donation, to the Safety Systems Foundation. He gave nothing to the PSRI. The following year he made no contributions to either charitable trust.

The operation of both trusts is a closely guarded secret. The Safety Systems Foundation has just one board member—his sister Claire Nader. PSRI has three board members—Nader himself, a cousin, and her husband.

These foundations exist ostensibly in order to donate

to charitable causes, namely Nader's own nonprofit organizations. But according to filings with the IRS, both of his foundations give only the bare minimum necessary to maintain their tax-exempt status. The rest is rolled into investments in corporate stock. For example, between 1997 and 2001 (the most recent years available), the Safety Systems Foundation gave away barely 4 percent of its money each year. Instead, the corporate crusader kept more than $1.3 million in corporate stock, including IBM, General Electric, Union Planters Corporation, and Iomega. He held literally hundreds of thousands of dollars in high-tech companies such as CNET Networks, ACTV, and Palm. By far the largest holding for the SSF was a close to $300,000 stake in Verizon, the telecommunications and wireless giant.

Nader's PSRI was likewise making more money in stocks than it was giving away to charitable causes. To keep its tax-exempt status, the institute gave away barely 4 percent of its assets to charities, despite the fact that between 1996 and 2000 the value of the foundation nearly doubled, growing from $931,512 to more than $1.6 million. Here Nader owns shares in AT&T Wireless, Qwest Communications (founded, ironically enough, by billionaire conservative activist Philip Anschutz), BellSouth Corporation, Vodafone, and General Electric.

At the time Nader held these investments, he was speaking loudly about the need to break up Microsoft. Calling the company to task for what he called "arrogant and predatory business practices," he filed briefs, gave speeches, and campaigned on the idea. "We need to build on the lessons from the Internet and stop Microsoft's efforts to transform the Internet into a private network dominated by a single ruthless company." What he never told anyone was that his investment portfolio, including millions of dollars in high-tech firms, would be directly, and positively, affected by a Microsoft breakup. Through the Computer and Communications Industry Association, companies like Qwest, Verizon, and BellSouth were pushing the legal case against the software giant. Had Microsoft been broken up, Nader's personal portfolio would have benefited enormously.

Nader also took the position of Verizon and other companies in his stock portfolio on the issue of new copyright laws concerning the Internet. In 2002, Verizon and other telecommunications companies in which he held stock sent a phalanx of lobbyists to Washington to oppose the efforts of the entertainment industry to tighten copyright laws. Nader took the same position, saying that he supported "fair use" of copyrighted material, not new restrictions.[18] Again, his activism, had it succeeded, would have substantially enhanced his investment portfolio.

No one can know Nader's motivation for his activism or investment decisions. What we do know is that, over the last four decades, his corporate radicalism and his appetite for stocks have danced very closely together. Thus, when he was waging his public war against General Motors and the ill-fated Corvair in the 1960s and publishing a book attacking the company, he was quietly buying shares in the Ford Motor Company through a Washington, D.C., broker. When asked about the purchase by a reporter, his broker confirmed it but explained that the stocks were not for the consumer activist himself but for

"Nader's mother."[19] Likewise, in the 1970s, when PSRI was attacking chemical and oil companies, Nader was buying and selling shares in Monsanto and Texaco. In 1970, Nader's trading was so intense that the IRS accused him of "churning stocks," an activity contrary to the "charitable purposes" of his foundations. PSRI was fined more than $3,000.[20]

In other instances, Nader has invested in companies that stood to benefit from his activism. On August 1, 1973, for example, PSRI bought three hundred shares of Allied Chemical for more than $11,000. Allied Chemical was the primary manufacturer of airbags, which Nader and PSRI were then campaigning for. The next day, August 2, General Motors announced that it was going to install airbags as an option on its cars. Three months later he sold the shares for a 23 percent profit.[21]

In 1976, Nader and his supporters were going after Firestone, claiming that the Firestone 500, a steel-belted radial tire, was faulty. Nader's Center for Auto Safety met with members of the National Highway Transportation Safety Administration (NHTSA) and encouraged them to investigate the company. The feds did eventually go after Firestone and forced a recall. Interestingly enough, however, during this campaign against Firestone, Nader's foundation had more than $17,000 worth of stock in Goodyear, Firestone's prime competitor.[22]

In 1970, two American corporate giants, International Telephone and Telegraph (ITT) and Hartford Fire Insurance, were proposing a merger. In April of that year, Nader tried to block the merger by filing a fifty-page brief to the Connecticut insurance commissioner, whose approval was required. Two and a half weeks later, Nader's SSF invested almost $8,000 on a short sale of ITT stock. (They were betting that the stock would go down.) Six days later Nader's SSF realized a $700 gain and got out before the merger was approved.

In all of his investing over the years, it is impossible to find any evidence that Nader's message about the dangers of corporate America trickles down into his own investment choices. He has prattled on about the dangers of outsourcing, but owned sizable stakes in Cisco, Verizon, and other companies that outsource to the Third World. He has criticized military contractors but invested in them and held stakes in companies that resist labor unions or bar them altogether. Oil companies have appeared in his portfolio even though they despoil the environment. His latest cause, fighting globalization and free trade, also doesn't prevent him from owning companies that benefit enormously from international trade. Bottled water may be evil, but dividends from multinationals are to be embraced!

Along with his crusade against corporations, Nader has made himself a champion for the working masses. Over the course of three decades he has been a tireless crusader on behalf of labor unions, safe working conditions, restrictions on the length of the workday, workers' rights, and "democratization" of the workplace. Some of his affiliate organizations, like Citizens for Tax Justice, have received huge grants from organized labor. Union officials have even served on the board of Citizen Action.

In his book *Big Boys,* Nader declares that labor unions are a "vital force in the battle over ideas, values and social conditions." Without them, he warns, American workers are on their way "to indentured status."[23] To protect workers from overbearing bosses out to exploit them, he has pushed for decades for what he calls an Employee Bill of Rights, including guarantees of free speech, privacy, and of course the right to organize. He also inveighs against employee surveillance techniques like hidden monitors and efficiency checklists as being "morally repugnant." This bill of workers' rights "is an essential corollary of democracy." During the 2000 campaign, Nader said that he favored unions even for small businesses with less than twelve employees. He also wants to protect "whistle-blowers" who bring abuses to light and envisions a truly democratic workplace with shared responsibility among all employees, not dictatorial managers and executives who don't pay attention to workers.

But he doesn't have any interest in those sorts of principles being applied at his own organizations. Tim Sharrock found that out when, as editor of the Nader publication *Multinational Monitor,* he tried to organize the staff because of difficult working conditions. Complaining of sixty- to eighty-hour workweeks and low pay (Sharrock, at the high end, was being paid $13,000 a year) as well as no procedure to address workplace grievances, they approached Nader about obtaining some sort of representation. Nader simply refused. "I don't think there is a role for unions in small nonprofit 'cause' organizations any more than . . . within a monastery or within a union," Nader said.

When employees tried to assert democracy at the workplace, Nader sounded like an old-line industrialist.

Because he was funding the publication, that gave him final control. (So much for workplace democracy.) A complaint went to the National Labor Relations Board, and Nader dealt with the problem by transferring ownership of the publication to his cousin, thereby avoiding any scrutiny. Sharrock was fired and the locks were changed on the office door. An effort to organize at Public Citizen, another Nader outfit, ended in a similar fashion.[24]

Despite his talk about workplace democracy, Nader doesn't have much interest in it when it comes to his own organizations. Although several of his groups are "membership" organizations, Nader rules them with an iron fist. Unlike the National Rifle Association, for example, which allows members to pick the board and establish organizational rules, "members" of Nader groups don't get any democratic rights.

Nader has also campaigned on the importance of employers providing mandatory health insurance, but don't expect it if you work for him yourself. Over the course of the past thirty years, many Nader employees have been hired as consultants, thereby allowing him to avoid the thorny and expensive matter of providing benefits. Nader has also been less than interested in complaints made about working conditions. When an "office revolt" occurred at one point in the 1970s, he agreed to meet with the employees to discuss their grievances, but scheduled the meeting for 7 A.M., an hour when few could be expected to show up. Former employee Dick Downy says that he was "glad to be out of that tight-assed operation. I think everyone was a little tired of the workload."

Jim Turner, another longtime employee, called the organization a "sweatshop." Nader paid small salaries and expected employees to shoulder a constant workload. "We spent a hundred years trying to clean sweatshops out of our system and what happens? Along comes the first major reformer of any impact, and he starts doing the same goddamned thing."

Nader also declared that marriages in his shop were "a problem" and actually discouraged his minions from tying the knot. He figured marriages would mean that employees would ask for more pay and be unwilling to work longer hours. Lowell Dodge, one of his most loyal lieutenants, said that working for Nader was terrible for marriages because of Nader's insistence that his people keep working eighty hours a week. "There is a gap between what you would expect from someone who is fighting to make the world a better place to live and what you actually get working on Nader's team," he observed. The writer James Fallows, who once worked on the Congress Project, said, "Ralph was very upset when I got married, because that's one step away from having the right devotion."[25]

Nader established a policy of requiring employees to keep a daily log accounting for their time. The form he created asked for information concerning all of their activities from seven in the morning until nine at night. If they failed to fill out the forms properly, Nader would not pay them. All this from the man who says that because corporate America is not democratic enough, it is leading to an alienated and disillusioned workforce.[26]

On a personal level, Nader may be the spartan moralist he claims to be, avoiding the lavish lifestyles of comrades in arms like Michael Moore. But in the end, he puts his faith in corporations and behaves like a traditional sweatshop boss. Co-ops and unions are great; but when you are trying to create a revolution, you are better off investing in corporations and working your employees to the bone.

▶▶ *NANCY PELOSI*

Ecological Scofflaw, Out-of-Touch Elitist, and Immigrant Labor Exploiter

In American politics today, it is hard to find a national political figure who will proudly carry the liberal label. Hillary Clinton, Al Gore, and John Kerry have all run away from it, preferring "moderate" or even "progressive" to describe their worldview. But Congresswoman Nancy Pelosi has it firmly pinned to her lapel. "I pride myself in being called a liberal," she told one reporter. "I don't consider myself a moderate."[1]

Matched with her unabashed liberalism is a solid reputation as a fighter. The leader of congressional Democrats has called President George W. Bush incompetent and declared that Republicans aren't concerned about poverty. When she disagreed with the Boy Scouts on their policy toward homosexuals, she tried to pass legislation preventing them from using public facilities such as schools for their activities. Her fighting spirit led some in her party to consider her a solid choice for the vice presidential slot in the 2004 election.

Pelosi's rise in national politics has been nothing short of meteoric. Nancy D'Alesandro grew up in a political family in the Little Italy section of Baltimore. Her father, congressman and Baltimore mayor "Big Tommy" D'Alesandro, was more than a politician—he was a political "boss," according to his daughter. The *National Catholic Reporter* called his operation "one of the great political machines of the century."[2] The garbage collectors might have been controlled by the mob, but Big Tommy saw to it that the trash always got picked up. Potholes got filled and the buses ran on time.

Big Tommy, with his thin mustache and pinky ring, would hold court at his house, handing out favors, forging alliances, and destroying political enemies all in one day. His machine was so effective that Big Tommy was later replaced by "Little Tommy," his son, who served as mayor in the 1960s. Nancy remembers being part of the family machine even on the schoolyard. When kids came to her needing a favor, "I would tell them how to get a sick relative into City Hospital, how to get a job that paid a living wage," she later recalled.[3]

Nancy went to college in Washington, D.C., and met a Georgetown student named Paul Pelosi, scion of another Italian-American political family, from California. After college, the two married and moved to New York City, where Paul worked as an investment banker until they headed back to his native San Francisco in 1969. In the

Bay area they became heavily involved in the real estate business.

As her husband expanded their business empire, Nancy dived into politics. Allying herself with liberal congressman Phil Burton, she became a prolific campaign fund-raiser. Using her husband's connections in the world of finance, real estate, and California politics, she raised money for liberal Democrats like Burton, Gov. Jerry Brown, and Dianne Feinstein. She advocated for campaign finance reform, but was a master practitioner of the art. The day after a federal judge declared unconstitutional a California law limiting campaign contributions, Pelosi sent a letter to supporters and members of the state delegation announcing the "good news"—while hitting them up for ten-thousand-dollar contributions. Little surprise that by 1981 she was chairman of the California Democratic Party.[4]

In 1985 she made a bid to become chairman of the Democratic National Committee. Facing Paul Kirk, an ally of House Speaker Tip O'Neill, she ran a spirited race. In the end she lost when labor lined up behind Kirk. Pelosi later claimed that labor leaders ran a sexist campaign against her. One labor leader famously called her "an airhead."

Pelosi first ran for elective office in 1987 when she was forty-seven years old. Congresswoman Sala Burton (widow of Congressman Phil Burton) had taken over her husband's congressional seat when he died in 1984. Three years later, dying in a hospital bed, she gave Pelosi her blessing to seek the seat. Overnight Pelosi raised hundreds of thousands of dollars. She won her first election and never looked back.

In Congress, Pelosi gave life to the term "San Francisco Democrat." When she first ran for office, it was on a platform of environmentalism and nuclear disarmament. She supported efforts to prevent the U.S. battleship *Missouri* from docking in San Francisco harbor with nuclear weapons aboard. She sponsored legislation to mandate that the U.S. Olympic Committee allow gays to hold athletic competitions under the term "Gay Olympics." When the Gulf War broke out, she attacked then-president Bush for "resorting to militarization in order to solve a conflict" and said he was acting "illegally." When Congress pushed for welfare reform and Bill Clinton signed the legislation, it was with strong opposition from Pelosi. When the Senate Foreign Relations Committee decided that it would not vote on a proposed International Treaty on Women, Pelosi went up to Chairman Jesse Helms and disrupted a meeting of the Foreign Relations Committee to publicly demand a hearing. Helms had her ejected by security.[5]

A member of the so-called Progressive Caucus, Pelosi is one of the most liberal members of Congress. Over the course of her career, she has garnered near-perfect ratings from the AFL-CIO, Americans for Democratic Action, and Planned Parenthood. In 2003 she tried to enshrine her philosophy by creating the so-called Center for Public Service and the Common Good at the University of San Francisco. (The Center is headed by Leo McCarthy, her longtime campaign treasurer, and funded by a $1 million federal grant she secured.)

In 2002, Pelosi became a national figure when her Democratic colleagues in the House selected her over a more moderate Steny Hoyer to lead their party in Congress.

Pelosi touts herself as a proud environmentalist. When members of the Rainforest Action Network and Project Underground were arrested for civil disobedience and faced charges of felony criminal mischief, it was Nancy Pelosi who wrote a testimonial asking that all charges be dismissed.[6] The League of Conservation Voters gives her a 90 percent approval rating. Her web site proudly declares: "Protecting the environment is vital to protect the health of all Americans, particularly our children. Democrats are fighting for cleaner air, cleaner water, and preservation of our natural resources, understanding that what we do today has an impact on future generations of Americans." She chides Republicans and corporations for harming the environment because of their greed and lack of interest in the concerns of the middle class. "With us," says Pelosi, "the environment is not an issue, it's an ethic, it's a value." The Pelosis even lease office space in one of their commercial buildings to the environmental group Sustainable Conservation.

Pelosi is also one of the most vocal class warriors in American politics today. In almost twenty years in Washington, she never seems to shy away from castigating her opponents as being unconcerned about the middle class and the poor. Republicans, she insists, are concerned only about the rich.

In short, it's hard to find a Democrat who more fully embraces the entire gamut of liberal politics, from soup to left-wing nuts. The question is, how well does her private conduct match up with her public ideals? The answer is, not very well at all. In fact, far from acting in accordance with her professed principles, Pelosi in fact epitomizes the very attitudes and practices she claims to detest.

Nancy Pelosi is one of the wealthiest members of Congress. (House Speaker Dennis Hastert, for example, is worth less than $1 million. Pelosi is worth more than $50 million.) According to her financial disclosure statements, one of her largest investments is a private partnership called Lions Gate Limited. The Pelosis have approximately $1 million in this golf development partnership, which operates the CordeValle Golf Club and Resort in San Martin, California. But how the club got established and how it has wiggled out of its environmental regulatory obligations tells us something about how thin Pelosi's commitment to her causes really is.

In 1996 a small group of investors was granted a use permit by the Santa Clara County Planning Commission to build a 275-acre golf course and resort in a beautiful valley thirty minutes south of San Jose. The permit was granted with some reluctance because of environmental and public concerns. To get the permit, Lions Gate Limited made several commitments to the county. For one thing, the partners promised to build "a public course," one where "60 percent of the total rounds (on an annual basis) will be reserved for public use." Note well: That's more than half of the projected golf course usage. Furthermore, in order to allay concerns about a threat to several endangered species, Lions Gate also agreed to abide by several environmental requirements in order to ensure that there would be minimal ecological damage.

The CordeValle Golf Course opened in 2000 to considerable fanfare. The Robert Trent Jones Jr.-designed course was called one of the best in the area. When the lodge opened in 2002, it boasted gorgeous bungalows, an exclusive restaurant, and one of the best wine lists in California. The club offered private memberships at $250,000 a pop. (Corporations paid $400,000.) The partners made enormous sums of money as the wealthy entrepreneurs of Silicon Valley rushed to enroll.

Then the Planning Commission started looking at what had actually been built. For starters, instead of honoring its commitment to build a fully public course, in practice it was nearly impossible for the general public to gain access. The club's rules were obviously intended to discourage outside use: Nonmembers needed to call seventy-two hours in advance, and the fee was $275 for eighteen holes. Even so, one board member discovered that a phone call would often yield the response "I'm sorry, we're full" even when the course was relatively empty. When the Planning Commission investigated the discrepancy, they found that perhaps only a dozen nonmembers had actually been able to play the course since it opened in 2000. When the commission requested an explanation, Lions Gate claimed that guests of its exclusive members should be counted as "the public."

The Planning Commission wasn't buying this and convened a series of public hearings to determine whether it should revoke the golf club's use permit. Barry Witt, a golf columnist for the *San Jose Mercury News,* concluded that the club was in clear violation and should be forced to live up to its commitment. What was supposed to be a largely public course was in fact a private one.[7]

Lions Gate had also agreed to several environmental protection provisions when they were granted the permit back in 1996. (Pelosi herself, of course, has been a long-time supporter of efforts to protect endangered species from development.) To its dismay, the commission found that the club had "ignored" many of its permit requirements. One of these was a commitment to provide habitat for two threatened species that would be displaced by the golf course: the California tiger salamander and the Western pond turtle. Lions Gate Limited had agreed in 1996 to build a series of ponds for these two endangered species—but it was now 2003 and none had been built. In addition, the Department of Fish and Game reported that Lions Gate had submitted only one of the required annual environmental reports in the last seven years. To make matters worse, the course was causing a drawdown in the freshwater aquifer, which could have serious implications for wildlife in the area.[8]

The San Jose Planning Commission issued a staff report in the summer of 2003 suggesting that it needed to seriously look at whether Lions Gate had engaged in "fraud" by making promises that it appeared to have had no intention of keeping.[9]

Facing charges that the public was being excluded from what was supposed to be a semipublic course and a clear record of not following environmental regulations, the Pelosis and their partners decided to solve the problem the old-fashioned way: They hired some wired-in lobbyists. A former San Jose City Council member and the campaign treasurer for the mayor were put on the payroll to work things out with the Planning Commission. The commission caved and simply asked Lions Gate to hold an annual charity golf tournament for children.

Four years after the course opened, it had still failed to deal with the environmental compliance issues. A November 2004 county report complained about how "improperly abandoned wells" were causing "water quality degradation"; how "urban pollutants" from the golf course were going into nearby Llagas Creek because they had not complied with required stormwater controls; and how the promised ponds for the salamanders and turtles had still not been built.[10]

If you visit CordeValle today, you still won't find many of those middle-class Americans Pelosi claims to be fighting for hacking away on the beautiful fairways. Instead you'll find "limousines and expensive sports cars" parked out front, as one profile of the course put it. And don't bother looking for any tiger salamanders or Western pond turtles. Our web-footed friends are largely gone, too.

Pelosi's office staffers won't answer any questions about CordeValle. They contend that this is a private matter. Well, sure it is. But isn't it important to know whether Pelosi's private conduct bears any relation to her publicly stated ideals? Perhaps the environmentalist group Bluewater Network should reconsider its decision to grant Pelosi its 2004 Environmental Leadership Award. "In San Francisco, the environment is a core value, not just an issue," she told them last September.[11] Evidently she feels quite confident in her ability to get away with such glaring hypocrisy—and she's right. The liberal press won't touch her.

Pelosi clearly relishes her role as the nation's moral

conscience, excoriating corporations for their neglect of the poor and middle class. She has written President Bush urging him to force American companies "to do more in affordable housing."[12] She expresses anger at the export of "manufacturing jobs" to foreign countries by profit-minded corporations more interested in their bottom line than in sustaining healthy communities at home. Outsourcing is a travesty, she says, because "all American workers deserve a chance at the American dream." But while Pelosi likes to talk about these values and wants to force others to act on them, she and her husband show no inclination to live by these dictates themselves.

In addition to their investment in Lions Gate, the Pelosis have an extensive investment portfolio, including stocks, real estate, and resorts. None of them are remotely concerned with increasing affordable housing or keeping blue-collar jobs in the United States.

A look at the Pelosis' investment pattern over the past five years reveals not a single manufacturing company. Instead, their multimillion-dollar portfolio includes extensive holdings in high-tech companies like Cisco, which not only outsources production to Asia but has recently created a business services division that will teach other companies to do the same. They also own shares in Sun Microsystems, Apogee Networks, Netclerk, and a quarter million dollars in Robert Half International, a temp agency. In all, their portfolio includes dozens of stocks, but it's hard to find one company that does not outsource. Equally rare: a company that boasts a unionized workforce.

The Pelosis' portfolio reveals another interesting fact.

Beacon Education Management is a contractor that provides educational services to traditional public schools and charter schools. As of 2004 it managed twenty-five charter schools in five states and the District of Columbia. The National Education Association hates organizations like Beacon because they function outside the orbit of teachers' unions and take tax dollars away from public schools. Nancy Pelosi gets a 100 percent approval rating from the National Education Association because of her opposition to charter schools and school vouchers. She wants money to go to public schools rather than into school reforms that she considers "risky." But that hasn't prevented the Pelosis from taking a $100,000 stake in Beacon Education Management. Indeed, the NEA might be interested to know that in a 2001 Securities and Exchange Commission filing, Paul Pelosi was listed as an officer of the company.

The Pelosis are also major players in the San Francisco area real estate market. They have close to $10 million in numerous real estate trusts and own several buildings outright. These holdings are all in exclusive areas of the city—Broadway, Point Lobos, Belden Place. The Pelosis own a house in the Silverado Country Club in Napa, an exclusive property that features neighbors like golfer Tom Kite. They also have a townhouse in Norden, California, that they rent for a considerable sum. Nary a one could be considered "affordable housing." Instead, these are expensive properties that pull in large rents from law firms, medical practices, and high-tech businesses. The closest the Pelosis get to investing in affordable housing is renting office space through their Borel Estate Company to the San Mateo County "Children and Family First Commission" for $44,500 a year.[13]

Nancy Pelosi made clear the extent of her commitment to "affordable housing" back in 1994. At that time there was a heated debate in San Francisco and Washington about the fate of the Presidio, the former military facility near the bay that was being closed by the Pentagon. The land was being given to the National Park Service, but what to do with it was open to question. The Presidio marks the most beautiful natural landscape left in a crowded San Francisco. Some Bay Area activists wanted to preserve the base and turn some of the barracks and other buildings into affordable housing. Many environmentalists initially lined up with them, asking that the current structures be left standing, with nothing new to be built on the property.

Developers believed this would be a waste of the land and that turning it into low-income housing might even depress property values in the surrounding neighborhoods. Pelosi, always the staunch environmentalist with a commitment to the poor, lined up with the developers. She wrote the legislation that allowed the Presidio to be privatized and converted into a real estate complex. Instead of affordable housing for the poor, she envisioned a complex "committed to education, environmental, and global issues," a sort of left-wing Disneyland. It should also be noted that the Pelosis own several real estate investments near the Presidio: a building two blocks away on Broadway and another on Point Lobos.

Environmentalist groups concerned about excessive

development were offered (i.e., bought off with) plum leases on what would become some of the most desirable and expensive commercial real estate in San Francisco. One big winner was the Tides Foundation, famous for making grants to environmentalist and radical causes. Tides was given a cheap lease on more than seventy thousand square feet at the Presidio and created a for-profit subsidiary to lease space to others at the park. They called it the Thoreau Center, and soon they attracted groups like the Wilderness Society, the Institute for Global Communications, and the Energy Foundation. Some staff members of these groups were even invited to live in renovated apartments in the park. In one instance, the executive director of a local nonprofit got to move into a house on the Presidio. These nonprofit organizations now enjoy long-term, cheap leases on some of the most prime real estate in the world. "It's sort of a social-justice ivory tower," says the *San Francisco Bay Guardian*.[14]

And what about the Pelosis? Real estate records reveal that in 1997, shortly after the Tides Foundation opened the Thoreau Center, the Pelosis sold one of their commercial buildings a few blocks away for several million dollars. Had a bunch of homeless people moved into the Presidio, the result would have been quite different.

So much for providing affordable housing. What about Pelosi's avowed commitment to fair labor practices?

In early 2003, Nancy Pelosi stepped up to the podium to receive the Cesar Chavez Legacy Award from the Cesar E. Chavez Foundation. Chavez, of course, was the migrant worker and activist who founded the United Farm Workers. As a revered icon of the labor movement (and a hero to her many Hispanic constituents), Pelosi never misses an opportunity to praise him or encourage his canonization. Pelosi wants a national holiday honoring Chavez and has nominated him several times to receive the Congressional Gold Medal. She was a grand marshal of a large San Francisco parade marking his seventy-fifth birthday, and every year she issues a statement on that day. She has declared him "one of America's greatest advocates for justice and equality, and a model of service to others." She applauds his efforts "in achieving fair wages, pension benefits and medical coverage for hundreds of thousands of working families."[15]

Apparently, however, these fundamental rights do not apply to families that may be picking grapes in Pelosi's own vineyards. Congresswoman Pelosi and her husband own a vineyard in the Napa Valley, on Zinfandel Lane in St. Helena, worth almost $25 million. (They recently sold another eight-acre vineyard on Skellenger Lane.) This is prime grape-growing soil, and the Pelosis make good money from their harvest, between $200,000 and $2 million a year according to financial disclosures.

The Pelosis don't pick the grapes themselves, of course; they hire outside firms to handle it. In recent years they have used several different harvesters, but they all have something in common: None have contracts with the UFW. The Pelosis sell their grapes to the non-union wineries Liparita Cellars and Roche. (Some of these wines made with Pelosi cabernet sauvignon grapes sell for more than $100 a bottle in restaurants.) In recent years the Pelosis have also held stakes in two other wine enterprises—Ravenswood Winery and the Charlore Wine Group (a consortium of smaller growers). Neither of these makes the UFW list as a "union-label" company.

The Pelosis cannot be ignorant of this. They are very familiar with the wine industry and Pelosi herself is well acquainted with Cesar Chavez's story. The fact that they don't insist on UFW labor when making their wine investments or picking their grapes tells us what they really think of him.

Pelosi has made supporting labor unions a cornerstone of her public career. She says unions are absolutely necessary because "collective bargaining efforts . . . have been so effective in promoting a balanced, cooperative relationship between labor and management."[16] She is a regular fixture at labor meetings and appears onstage at the AFL-CIO meeting every year as a keynote speaker. In 2004 she made a point of saying, "Thank you all for fighting for America's working families. And thank you for fighting to end the union-busting, family-hurting, exporting jobs presidency of George W. Bush."[17] Needless to say, organized labor has been the largest source of Pelosi's campaign funds in the last three elections, offering up a total of $769,000 in PAC contributions.

Pelosi supported the Employee Free Choice Act to encourage union membership and has a 96 percent lifetime rating from the AFL-CIO. She supported the grocery workers when they held a strike recently in California. When a hotel strike erupted in San Francisco, Pelosi scolded the hotel industry for stonewalling. San Francisco, she said, "has a long history of organized labor negotiating good wages and working conditions for workers and their families."[18] She has been a supporter of the AFL-CIO's Hotel Employees and Restaurant Employees (HERE) efforts to organize around the country, and they have been financial contributors to her campaigns. In the last three campaigns, the HERE PAC has given her $20,000—more than it has given to any other congressional candidate.

In addition to the wine business, the Pelosis are also involved in the hotel and restaurant business. Not surprisingly, their lack of personal commitment to hiring union labor in the vineyards is matched by their anti-union position at their hotels and eateries.

The Pelosis own a large stake in an exclusive, fifty-room hotel and resort in Napa, California. Auberge du Soleil features a world-class French restaurant, a luxury spa, and beautiful rooms and cottages, all in the ambience of Provence. A stay at this hillside perch overlooking the Napa Valley does not come cheap. The smallest room will run you $450 a night, and cottages fetch $3,500. (But don't bring the kids—no one under sixteen is allowed.) The hotel resort has more than fifty rooms and boasts more than 250 employees—but it is a strictly nonunion shop. The dishwashers, maid staff, busboys, and bellboys (many of them Hispanic immigrants) might be targeted in membership drives by HERE, but at Auberge they will have to face management alone. In Washington and on the stump, Pelosi seems greatly interested in the fate of hotel and restaurant employees. But if the union tried to organize at Auberge, they would be shown the door. "Things are fine the way they are," one manager said to me before he hung up.

Until recently, the Pelosis were also partners in another exclusive hotel, the San Ysidro Ranch in Santa Barbara. Naturally, it is nonunion, too.

When I called Pelosi's congressional office, the press operation had no comment on this glaring inconsistency. But her web site does make it clear that she's very upset at her political opponents who are always "rewarding wealth over work and putting profits before people."[19]

I should add one bit of personal advice: Representative Pelosi should not plan on convening a retreat or leadership meeting with labor leaders at Auberge. The AFL-CIO leadership has a policy of staying only in hotels that hire union help.

In addition to the tony Napa Valley resort, the Pelosis are also partners in a restaurant chain called Piatti. (Based on her financial disclosure form, the family's stake is somewhere between $5 million and $25 million.) The chain boasts sixteen restaurants in five states and has more than nine hundred employees. Dine there and you can feast on veal and mushroom stew or handkerchief pasta. But work there bussing tables, washing dishes, serving guests, or preparing food, and you can't get a union card. As with Auberge du Soleil, at Piatti the Pelosis' commitment to organized labor ends at the front door.

It is interesting to take note that all of the Pelosis' largest investments—the vineyard, the hotels, and the restaurants—make use of immigrant labor, those most vulnerable to labor exploitation. Pelosi favors liberal immigration laws and amnesty for illegals already here. Her position perfectly fits the Pelosis' financial interests.

Noam Chomsky and Michael Moore have their hypocrisies, but they are persuaders and critics at best. What makes Pelosi a particularly galling example of do-as-I-say liberalism is that she not only acts hypocritically, she legislates that way, too. Not content with simply trying to persuade other people to see things her way, she wants to compel them to embrace her ideas through law. Ironically, that is the only way she will ever be forced to practice what she preaches.

▶▶ *GEORGE SOROS*

Inside Trader, Economic Globalist, Corrupting Financial Influence

There is a loud new voice on the left, and he speaks with a Hungarian accent. And unlike Ralph Nader, Hillary Clinton, or others profiled in this book, he prefers to work largely behind the scenes. But his influence is perhaps greater than all of theirs.

George Soros is one of the world's richest men, with a net worth north of $7 billion. And he has become a major player on the national political stage. "We need people like George Soros, who is fearless and willing to step up when it counts," Hillary Clinton said recently.

When Soros "steps up," it usually means whipping out his checkbook. During the Cold War, he sent millions of dollars to dissident groups behind the Iron Curtain. After the Curtain fell, he provided hundreds of millions in aid to the postcommunist countries. For these activities he earned the respect of many in the United States and Europe.

But in recent years, Soros has embraced many of the tenets of the political far left. He has given money to *The Nation* magazine, *Mother Jones,* and the Feminist Majority Foundation. In 2003 he gave $5 million to MoveOn.org and another $10 million to Americans Coming Together in an urgent crusade to defeat George W. Bush, whom he believed represented a fundamental threat to global peace. In the six months before the election, Soros traveled the country, speaking on college campuses and to the media about the need to defeat Bush. He did so with the authority that comes from being perceived as a self-made billionaire with a social conscience.

America under Bush "is a danger to the world," Soros said in an interview with the *Washington Post.* He likened Vice President Dick Cheney, Attorney General John Ashcroft, and Defense Secretary Donald Rumsfeld to Yasser Arafat and compared Bush himself to the Nazis. "When I hear Bush say, 'You're either with us or against us,' it reminds me of the Germans," he told the *Post.* "My experiences [in Hungary] under Nazi and Soviet rule have sensitized me." Under Bush, civil rights would "disappear," Soros claimed. He seemed particularly concerned that Bush was acting out of some misguided messianic impulse: "Bush feels that on September 11 he was anointed by God. He's leading the U.S. and the world toward a vicious circle of escalating violence." If Bush won, Soros said, he planned to go away to "some kind of monastery to reflect on what is wrong with us."

Bush, of course, won reelection, and though Soros did

not withdraw to a monastery, he was certainly befuddled. He is a man not used to losing. In much of the rest of the world he is feared because he usually gets what he wants. In China they call him "the Crocodile." In Chinese lore, the crocodile elicits particular fear because it is ruthless and has a voracious appetite. It's an identity Soros enjoys. During a recent visit there he joked, "Watch out, the crocodile is coming."[1]

Like many other wealthy men, Soros fancies himself a philosopher and travels the world preaching his own eccentric gospel, based on the ideas developed by Karl Popper in *The Open Society*—a society that would "maximize the freedom of individuals to live as they wish." He also touts an esoteric idea of "equilibrium" that even his friends and associates seem not to understand. Soros speaks with such religious zeal that it prompted one journalist to suggest he be appointed pope. "Why?" he responded. "I'm the pope's boss now." Soros's God complex is a matter of public record. Indeed, while charging that Bush's religious faith makes him mentally unfit for office, Soros has himself admitted to messianic impulses. "I fancied myself as some kind of god," Soros once said. On other occasions he's noted, "If the truth be known, I carried some rather potent messianic fantasies with me from childhood, which I felt I had to control, otherwise they might get me in trouble." But he has apparently come to terms with the problem. "It is a sort of disease when you consider yourself some kind of god, the creator of everything, but I feel comfortable about it now since I began to live it out."[2]

The invocation of the divine is not some idle fancy on

Soros's part. Like Chomsky, Moore, and Nader, Soros speaks in high-flown moral platitudes and not only claims to have discovered the Truth, but expects others to follow his precepts. But if Soros's example teaches us anything, it's that a very wealthy man with plenty of influence really believes that the rules other people have to follow do not apply to him.

Soros's moral stature on the left comes from the fact that he made money as a capitalist and has now seemingly converted to the leftist cause. This reformed capitalist billionaire now wants to fight capitalism, reverse globalism, and soak the rich with steep income and inheritance taxes. He also wants to legalize drugs, promotes unfettered immigration, and advocates euthanasia and assisted suicide. Among his other causes are abortion rights, atheism, sex education, gun control, and gay marriage. To advance his agenda, he has given tens of millions of dollars to the Democratic Party and organizations that support liberal/left causes.

Who is this man who postures as a public benefactor and global philosopher, who fancies himself a seer and prophet, a Moses pointing the way to a Promised Land of progressive social engineering?

Soros was born George Schwartz in 1930 to a Jewish family in Hungary. His father Tivador was a lawyer/publisher who changed the family name to Soros in 1936. "Soros grew up in a family that was so detached from its Jewish roots," summarized a *Business Week* review of his biography, "that they even vacationed in Nazi Germany, with Tivador shrugging off 'No Jews Allowed' signs by telling his wife, 'You are a foreigner, it's not for you.'"

When the Germans invaded Hungary, the family lived in fear that their Jewish roots would be discovered. Soros survived the horrors of Nazi-occupied Europe. But he did so by using a method that few others dared to try. During the occupation the family split up, and George, then fourteen, assumed the identity of a Gentile boy named Sandor Kioo. The man who acted as his surrogate father was no ordinary Hungarian. His job was to confiscate the property of Hungarian Jews and turn it over to the Germans. As Soros said in an April 15, 1993, interview on European television, "I actually went with him, and we took decisions on these large estates. That was my identity." Soros told one interviewer that 1944 Hungary occupied by the Nazis was "in many ways . . . the happiest year of my life."[3]

After the war came the Soviet occupation, and young George managed to slip through the Iron Curtain and landed penniless in London. As a poor young man, he tried to get a Jewish charity to give him money while also receiving public assistance. When the charity refused, Soros was furious. This is ironic, since, as Joshua Muravchik points out, he was essentially trying to perpetrate a fraud by double-dipping and not disclosing his pension.[4] Soros went on to study at the London School of Economics and eventually migrated to the United States, where he began a career in currency speculation and trading.

There is no question that when it comes to speculating on currency values, Soros has the magic touch. When he established the Quantum Fund in 1973, he began with just a few million in assets. By 1985, Quantum was worth more than $1 billion. Today the fund's value is over $10 billion. Over the course of his twenty-year stewardship, Quantum has returned a spectacular 34.5 percent per year. If you had invested $1,000 with Soros in 1969, today it would be worth more than $2 million. His timing often seems perfect and his choices uncannily prescient.

The Left's embrace of Soros is easy to understand given his devotion to their favorite causes and the fact that he is critical of capitalism. He especially opposes what he calls "market fundamentalism," that is, capitalism as it is practiced today. He has gone so far as to say that capitalism "is today a greater threat to open society than any totalitarian ideology."[5] He also sees merit in the Marxist critique of capitalism. "The owners of capital seek to maximize their profits. Left to their own devices, they would continue to accumulate capital until the situation became unbalanced."[6] Complaining about "the heedless pursuit of profit," he calls on people to pay more in taxes and give up their greedy ambitions. "We must put the common interest ahead of our individual self-interest even if others fail to do so. That is the only way the common interest can prevail."[7]

Those are high-sounding words. But while Soros repeats them ad nauseam, he actually does the exact opposite.

To begin with, currency speculation is a particularly predatory form of capitalism. Most forms of capitalism include voluntary exchange. Bill Gates, for example, has made billions because people chose to spend their money on Microsoft products. In currency speculation you profit by betting that others will lose large sums of money.

When a nation's currency crashes, hurting an entire country, Soros makes billions.

Soros also plays the game in other ways. For example, he has been known to quietly "short" a currency (betting that it will go lower) and then publicly state that it will drop. When Soros speaks, people listen, and the currency does often drop. He then sells for a tidy profit. As the Banker for International Settlements noted in one annual report, big investors who do this "can more often than not make that view self-fulfilling."[8] This is not illegal because Soros established Quantum (and all of his other funds) offshore, meaning that he is not subject to Security and Exchange Commission (SEC) rules.

In 1992 he made perhaps his boldest move when he sold British pounds sterling short against the deutsche mark. He bet $10 billion on the pound, and when it went reeling, Soros walked away with a cool $1 billion in one day. The cost to the British taxpayer and economy was enormous.

The drop in the British pound aroused European concerns about other currencies. On July 26, 1993, Soros published a letter in the French paper *Le Figaro* promising that he would not speculate against the French franc because he did not want to be blamed for destroying the European monetary system. Suddenly everyone was paying attention to the franc, and it did indeed drop. Soros did not have any options on the franc, but he did have a bundle on the Danish kroner. The franc's woes lead to the kroner's increase and he was able to reap another windfall.[9]

In May 1998 the Russian ruble came under what the *Wall Street Journal* called "a heavy assault by financial speculators led by Soros." Within a month the Russian economy was on the brink of collapse. Millions of workers went unpaid, soldiers were being fed pet food, and pensioners faced the prospect of a winter without any income. This happened at the very moment when Soros was lecturing other capitalists on the need to "put the common good over our personal self-interest."

The Thai baht caught Soros's attention a few months later. Although the Thai government tried to shore up the currency, it was in the end forced to devalue, sending shock waves throughout the fast-growing Asian economies. Currencies fell and businesses throughout the region collapsed. After the dust settled, Soros reentered the market by purchasing Korean factories and infrastructure at bargain basement prices.[10]

As a result, the name Soros evoked outrage across Asia. Malaysian prime minister Mahathir Mohamad declared that he was one of those "rich people from rich countries" who "have no compunction about impoverishing the poor in order to enrich themselves." He also made some anti-Semitic remarks about "Jewish bankers" having too much power.[11] The mayor of Bangkok asked: "Doesn't he feel ashamed, coming to see our misery which resulted from his sinister actions? He deserves a good bang on the head." A planned trip to Bangkok had to be canceled because of threatened protests and perhaps fears of a sore noggin.[12]

There is more than a bit of irony in the fact that a man who promotes an "open society" can operate in secrecy, manipulating the very international rules and regulations that he champions in order to enrich himself and his investors. Elected leaders who act unilaterally, like Bush, are dangerous. But unelected speculators like Soros, with his hypocritical calls for an open society, are free to compromise the economic health of entire countries.

Like many wealthy men, Soros has invested a good deal of effort to position himself as a philanthropist. But his philanthropic efforts to "open" developing countries and make them more free and transparent also serve his corporate interests. In Kosovo, for instance, where he has poured millions of dollars in aid, he has also invested $50 million in an effort to gain control of the state-owned Trepca mine complex, estimated to have reserves of gold, silver, and lead worth more than $5 billion. According to British journalist Neil Clark, Soros "thus copied a pattern he has deployed to great effect over the whole of Eastern Europe: of advocating shock therapy and economic reform, then swooping in with his associates to buy valuable state assets at knockdown prices."[13]

Sometimes his employees move to key positions elsewhere, with any resulting benefits going to Soros. When Arminio Fraga resigned from the Soros Foundation in 1999, he was appointed head of Brazil's Central Bank. Soros apparently bought huge amounts of Brazilian national debt at a discount shortly before the appointment took place. Fraga was working for Soros until the day before his appointment. Presumably Soros had some inkling of what Fraga might do, simply by knowing what his views were.[14] The actions of the Brazilian Central Bank greatly influence his large Latin American investments.

Soros's investment practices have also brought scrutiny. Several years ago he settled a stock manipulation charge brought by the U.S. government. The SEC said that Soros had driven down the price of a company called Computer Sciences a day before the public offering of the stock. The next day he was able to buy 165,000 shares "at artificially low prices."[15] In 2002, Soros was convicted of insider trading in France. He apparently bought stocks at the French bank Societe Generale with inside knowledge.[16]

The Soros philosophy on investing is clear and direct, says his former chief trader, Stanley Druckenmiller. "Soros has taught me that when you have tremendous conviction to a trade, you have to go for the jugular. It takes courage to be a pig."[17]

When Soros first began espousing these noble-sounding ideas in the mid-1990s, many saw in him what even liberal columnist Paul Krugman called "blinding hypocrisy." Sir Ralf Dahrendorf, a British historian who considers himself a personal friend of Soros, admits that the man wants to be "both poacher and gamekeeper. He likes to style himself as a benevolent bandit . . . he will continue to benefit from the capitalism which he professes to dislike." Britain's Lord Skidelsky concurs: "He is tirelessly telling the world it now needs to remove the ladder by which he himself climbed to fame and fortune."[18]

Soros himself admits: "I am the classic limousine liberal."[19]

The American left used to criticize Soros, as Krugman did in 1998 when he dismissed his ideas as "the lamentations of a rich man who's made his pile and can now afford the luxury of a social conscience."[20] Since then, Soros has poured hundreds of millions into the American left, and such criticisms have been replaced by adoration by the likes of *The Nation*, which never seems to have anything nice to say about any billionaires except this one.[21] (What's more, he has purchased this left-wing reputation at a fraction of the cost assumed by previous robber barons like Carnegie and Rockefeller.)

So Soros continues to decry greedy capitalists and their lack of a "social conscience." But when it comes to his own actions, he sings a different tune. Asked about his play against the British pound, Soros writes: "When I sold sterling short in 1992, the Bank of England was on the other side of my transactions and I was taking money out of the pockets of British taxpayers. But if I had tried to take the social consequences into account, it would have thrown off my risk/reward calculations and my chances of being successful would have been reduced." In an interview with *60 Minutes,* he declared: "I am basically [in business] to make money. I cannot and do not look at the social consequences of what I do." He never explains why he gets to play by a different set of rules than anybody else.[22]

Soros has also written about the need for stiffer corporate regulations, particularly when it comes to environmental standards, international financial transactions, and taxation. But when he appeared before the U.S. Congress to describe his role in the crash of the British pound, he opined that his own fund did not need regulating.[23]

When not trashing capitalism, Soros is decrying the

failure of the wealthy to pay more in taxes. He continues to advocate "higher taxes for the wealthy" and "more progressive taxation."[24] He has bankrolled organizations like the Institute on Taxation and Economic Policy, which pushes those ideas in Washington. He's particularly concerned that government's ability to provide for the welfare of its citizens "has been severely impaired by the ability of capital to escape taxation."[25]

But Soros himself is a master at evading taxation. While Soros maintains his office in New York, the Quantum Fund is actually incorporated in the tiny island of Curaçao in the Netherlands Antilles. As the manager of an offshore account, he is not required to register with the SEC. His ultrasecret, unregulated fund avoids not only the SEC but also public scrutiny. No one knows who his investors are, though many believe they include some of the wealthiest people in the world, including Saudi princes, royal families in Europe, and the superwealthy of Latin America. Even employees at Soros Fund Management in New York do not know the names of many of the people they are making millions for. They are simply given coded Swiss bank accounts.[26] The International Task Force on Money Laundering of the OECD (Organisation for Economic Co-Operation and Development) named this Caribbean tax haven as one of the largest money-laundering centers in the world for the Latin American drug trade.

Operating in the Netherlands Antilles also allows Soros to avoid paying taxes in the United States. Because there are no American members on his fund's board (which would trigger SEC involvement), Americans who invest in his funds can keep their money offshore and not pay a penny in taxes. Payments of dividends, interest, or capital gains will be taxed only if they are brought to the United States. Soros's funds benefited him early on because they were a tax-avoidance scheme: Even if similar funds in the United States offered a similar rate of return, those profits would be taxed. Little surprise that because of pioneer George Soros, offshore investment funds have become all the rage in recent years.

Offshore businesses that avoid taxation are a Soros specialty. In one of his more clever plays, Soros's real estate company, Mapeley Steps, bought more than six hundred buildings from Britain's Inland Revenue, their equivalent of the IRS. Soros then leased the buildings back to the British government for 220 million pounds. But Mapeley Steps doesn't pay taxes because the company is headquartered in Bermuda, another notorious tax haven. The irony was not lost on British members of Parliament, who noted that Soros was profiting from doing business with the British government without paying British taxes on those profits.[27]

Soros has also been vocal on another tax issue of interest to the liberal/left—the estate tax. In 2003, along with fellow billionaires Warren Buffett, Bill Gates, and others, he signed a public letter that stated, "Repealing the estate tax would enrich the heirs of America's millionaires and billionaires while hurting families who struggle to make ends meet." But Soros himself has figured out a way to beat the estate tax.[28]

Many commentators give Soros a sort of free pass on the taxation issue. After all, isn't he giving away large sums of money as a philanthropist? He is, but in typical fashion, Soros is exploiting a quirk in the American tax code that allows him to avoid paying estate taxes by doing so. As Soros explains it: "A charitable lead trust is a very interesting tax gimmick. The idea is that you commit your assets to a trust and you put a certain amount of money into charity every year. And then after you have given the money for however many years, the principal that remains can be left [to one's heirs] without estate or gift tax. So this was the way I set up the trust for my children." Call me narrow-minded, but shouldn't billionaires who support estate taxes for others be prepared to pay them?[29]

Soros has also banged the drum about the "military-industrial complex," which profits from war and exerts a distorting influence on American foreign policy. But that hasn't caused him to divest from his more than $100 million stake in the infamous Carlyle Group—one of America's largest military companies, often mentioned by the groups Soros funds as a major inspiration for the invasion of Iraq. He owns one of the biggest chunks of the company. (It is strange that when organizations such as MoveOn.org have attacked the Carlyle Group, they mention the names of others associated with the company, but not their benefactor Soros.) Soros has also tried to acquire other military companies, like Inmarsat, whose high-tech satellites were used extensively by the U.S. Navy during the Iraq War.[30]

When he's not decrying the evils of capitalism and the military-industrial complex, Soros positions himself as a supreme environmentalist. In addition to supporting radical environmentalist causes, he has criticized the exploitation of the developing world by rapacious multinational corporations who despoil the ecosystem, extract precious natural resources, and share none of the profits.

The Argentine beef industry is a prime example: It has been blamed by environmental activists for everything from polluting the country's water supply to causing extensive deforestation. But Soros himself is the biggest landowner in Argentina (half a million hectares) and has more than 150,000 head of cattle.[31] He's also part owner of Apex Silver Mines, which digs for treasure in a remote and ecologically sensitive area of Bolivia (but is registered in the Cayman Islands to avoid those pesky Bolivian taxes).[32]

Soros has also poured tens of millions of dollars into the cause of drug legalization. He credits the late poet Allen Ginsberg, whom he befriended in the 1980s, with enlightening him on the issue (and introducing him to marijuana). Since then he has given money to the Marijuana Policy Project, the Drug Policy Foundation, and the Lindesmith Center. Because of his largesse, Joseph Califano of Columbia University's National Center on Addiction and Substance Abuse calls him the "Daddy Warbucks of drug legalization."[33]

Along with billionaires Peter Lewis of Progressive Insurance and John Sperling of the online University of Phoenix, Soros has supported ballot initiatives on the legalization of marijuana in four states. Soros is on the outer fringes of the drug legalization movement in that he wants to see not only marijuana, but also harder drugs made legal. "I'll tell you what I would do if it were up to me," he says. "I would establish a strictly controlled distribution network through which I would make most drugs, excluding the most dangerous ones like crack, legally available."[34]

During an event at Washington's National Press Club in May 2004 where Soros spoke, protests were heard from parents who had lost children to drugs. Several of them held up pictures of their dead sons or daughters, and one of them asked Soros directly if he had ever lost a child to drug abuse. None of this affected Soros in the slightest—understandably, since Soros himself is well insulated from the social and personal ravages of America's drug problem. According to one African-American activist, "A month ago, we had a meeting at his estate—it was nice being up there: He has a beautiful home," she recalled. "That night—I live in Brooklyn near the projects—I heard gunshots. One thing I couldn't help thinking about is that [Soros] doesn't have that experience. He doesn't have to hear gunshots. The drug war has a different meaning for me."[35]

I tried to find out how Soros deals with drugs on a practical level. What is the substance abuse policy at his investment fund? What is the policy for those who work at his charities? Does he take a laissez-faire attitude toward consumption? After six phone calls and half a dozen e-mails, it became clear that no one wanted to give me an answer. A spokeswoman for the Open Society Institute said the question "wasn't funny." When I told her I wasn't joking, she said "no comment" and hung up.

What is Soros's policy? I'm assuming that he has taken the same approach as John Sperling, a fellow billionaire pushing for drug legalization. Sperling may want a laissez-faire policy for the country at large, but at the University of Phoenix both employees and students are under a "zero tolerance" policy. There is no mention in the school's public policy guidelines of drug counseling or second chances.

Why is Soros pushing for the legalization of drugs? One very possible answer is that he hopes to profit from them once they become legal. He has been particularly active in South America, buying up large tracts of land and forging alliances with those in a position to mass-produce narcotics should they be legalized in the United States. He has also helped fund the Andean Council of Coca Leaf producers. Needless to say, this organization would stand to benefit enormously from the legalization of cocaine. He has also taken a 9 percent stake in Banco de Colombia, located in the Colombian drug capital of Cali.[36] The Drug Enforcement Administration has speculated that the bank is being used to launder money and that Soros's fellow shareholders may be members of a major drug cartel.

Soros never gets called on any of this, of course, in part because many in the press share his agenda. His financial support of the Center for Public Integrity, a research organization popular with the mainstream media, no doubt gives him additional cover.

But Soros's most glaring act of hypocrisy is also his most glaringly self-serving. In the 1990s, Soros was a leading light in the movement for campaign finance reform. Through more than $18 million in contributions, Soros said he was determined to get rid of the "corrupting influence" of money on our politics. In addition to his direct support for ballot initiatives, Soros also underwrote all the groups pushing for new campaign finance laws. As a *Wall Street Journal* editorial noted, "Combine . . . the $1.7 million that Mr. Soros gave the Center for Public Integrity, the $1.3 million he gave Public Campaign, the $300,000 to Democracy 21, the $625,000 to Common Cause, and the $275,000 to Public Citizen—and you can be forgiven for believing Mr. Soros got campaign finance passed all by himself."

But even as he was underwriting the drive for campaign finance reform, he was already figuring ways to get around it. In the 2000 election he became one of the pioneers in funding and directing so-called 527 committees. He put together a team of wealthy Democratic donors and pushed two of his favorite issues—gun control and drug legalization. He personally gave $500,000 to the Campaign for a Progressive Future, which was pushing ballot initiatives to pass gun control legislation.

When the McCain-Feingold campaign finance reform bill became law in 2002, Soros jumped in to fill the void. He might have been critical of George W. Bush's contributions from wealthy individuals ("pioneers") or the National Rifle Association, but that didn't stop him from acting likewise on a much grander scale. On July 17, 2003, Soros assembled a group of major Democratic donors, strategists, and fund-raisers at his Southampton, New York, home. Guests included the head of the Sierra Club; former Clinton chief of staff John Podesta; the head of the feminist PAC Emily's List; fellow billionaire Peter Lewis; Rob Glaser, founder and CEO of RealNetworks; Rob McKay (Taco Bell); and Lewis and Dorothy Cullman, heirs to the Benson & Hedges tobacco fortune. This group of concerned citizens, who called themselves Americans Coming Together (ACT), pledged to pitch in $25 million to defeat Bush (with $10 million coming from Soros).

A few months later, Wes Boyd, head of the anti-Bush web site MoveOn.org, paid a visit to Soros. During this meeting the billionaire pledged $5 million to institute what he called "regime change" in the United States. Weeks later, Soros sat down with a *USA Today* reporter and declared his objective. Toppling Bush, he said, "is the central focus of my life...And I'm willing to put my money where my mouth is." Would Soros spend his entire $7 billion fortune to defeat Bush, the reporter asked? "If someone guaranteed it," Soros replied.[37]

According to the Center for Public Integrity, Soros gave in all an estimated $24 million to defeat Bush. Much of the money went for television ads denouncing Bush. Soros's son Jonathan personally oversaw MoveOn.org's television efforts, including the famous thirty-second spot contest in which one of the entries included comparisons of Bush to Hitler. In all, MoveOn.org used millions of Soros's money to buy television ads in so-called swing states. Yet when Soros was pushing campaign finance reform, he claimed that he wanted to "do something about...the distortion of our electoral process by the excessive use of TV advertising." In a very manipulative way, he did succeed by distorting political advertising in his favor. While the political parties were limited in the sorts of television advertisements they could run, and organizations such as the National Rifle Association faced restrictions, Soros-backed 527s did not.

How does Soros justify this kind of blatant hypocrisy? In typical fashion, he says that unlike anyone else, his injection of tens of millions into the political process serves the common good. "I am not motivated by self-interest but by what I believe to be the public interest. So when the Republican National Committee attacks me and distorts my motives. . . . You see, I'm different from their contributors."

A more plausible explanation comes from his own book, *Soros on Soros*. "I do not accept the rules imposed by others. . . . I am a law-abiding citizen, but I recognize that there are regimes that need to be opposed rather than accepted. And in periods of regime change, the normal rules don't apply." Clearly, Soros considers himself uniquely qualified to determine when the "normal rules" should and shouldn't apply.

The embrace of George Soros by many on the liberal-left is evidence of their desperation. Soros is nothing that he claims to be and is a walking contradiction of the values he claims to espouse. Very few people can take Soros's ideas seriously. Take away his money, and the liberal-left won't take him seriously, either.

▶▶ *BARBRA STREISAND*

Civil Liberties Violator, Outsourcer, War Profiteer

She has been called "the strongest political voice in Hollywood." She speaks about issues like the environment, poverty, and feminism with supreme confidence and moral certainty. When Bill Clinton was president, she not only raised millions of dollars for him, she practically lived in the Lincoln Bedroom and chatted with him frequently about policy matters.[1] In the 1990s, when Clinton was supposedly pushing his party to the center, Frank Rich of the *New York Times* called her the only public defender of liberalism in America. Some people appear to be listening. In Canada and the United States you can find "What Would Barbra Do?" T-shirts.[2]

Despite her affection for Clinton, Streisand has always been further to the left than he. *"The Nation* magazine," she told one reporter, "I love it. I keep every copy. I've never thrown one out. I keep them bound."[3]

Streisand grew up in relative poverty and adopted the politics of her late father and mother, who were staunch Democrats. But in the 1970s she moved further to the left. She embraced the feminism of Gloria Steinem and Betty Friedan, who became close friends and political allies. She also became a friend and ally of Bella Abzug, a congresswoman from New York with a radical hue to her politics. During Abzug's first campaign, Streisand held a massive fund-raiser for "that very special lady running for Congress who is dedicated to peace." Abzug won in part because of her extensive war chest.[4] Two years later Streisand was campaigning for George McGovern. She raised thousands of dollars for him at events in Los Angeles and was deeply distressed by his defeat. She didn't campaign for Jimmy Carter because she considered him "too conservative."

Streisand's emergence as a national player in the Democratic Party came in the mid-1980s, in the midst of Reaganism. How it happened reveals something about her politics and the hopeless simplicity of the way she views the world.

Shortly after the Chernobyl nuclear power plant spewed radioactive gas across Europe, Streisand called her close friend Marilyn Bergman. "[Barbra and I] were talking about the disaster at Chernobyl," Bergman recalled. "She called me that morning, and she was absolutely horrified at what happened. The question was, 'What can be done about this?' And the answer was, 'The only thing that I know to do about it is to take back the Senate for the Democrats.' "[5]

Streisand organized a concert at her compound in Malibu and the glitterati of Hollywood turned out. Streisand performed some of her classics for this very select audience. From the proceeds she established the Barbra Streisand Foundation, through which she would funnel millions of dollars to radical and liberal causes, including "antinuclear activities and the preservation of our environment, civil liberties and human rights." Unlike Michael Moore, whose foundation gives away the bare minimum necessary to maintain its tax exempt status, Streisand is the real deal, gung-ho to fund her causes. She gives away close to 30 percent of her foundation's assets to liberal causes every year—the Feminist Majority Fund, Rainforest Action Network, Environmental Defense Fund, the ACLU, and dozens more. She also helps raise funds for these organizations by holding concerts and making appearances.

Within the Democratic Party she has become a potent force because of the financial largesse she can tap by simply giving a concert. For Clinton she could raise millions in one night. (She also became the first Hollywood star to threaten to flee the country if President Bush was reelected—the first President Bush, back in 1992. Though things have clearly gone from bad to worse, she has yet to make good on her threat.)

Streisand has also sought to become a prominent spokeswoman for the Left, giving speeches and offering advice to political figures. Most famously, thanks to a leak in the Drudge Report, she sent a memo to then–House Leader Richard Gephardt that presumed to speak for "the working men and women of this country." Addressed to

Richard "Gebhardt," the error-filled memo included numerous misspellings, such as "Sadam Hussein," "Al Queda," and "our fingers holding the dyke [sic] against the Republic revolution." But the memo itself was taken seriously by numerous senior Democrats.

Today, Streisand is not only a national icon for the Left but an international one as well. When leftist strongman Hugo Chavez of Venezuela wanted international monitors to watch elections in his country, he asked Barbra to be one of them.[6]

But on the three causes with which Streisand seems most concerned—the struggle of the working class against the greed of the rich, environmentalism, and feminism—there is a yawning gap between what she says and what she actually does. After she pours her political moralism out for all to see, Streisand quietly returns to her cocoon of wealth and privilege and engages in the very behaviors she says she deplores.

Streisand has long carried a torch for the "working class," professing to be their proponent, friend, and champion. But speaking for the working class as a whole should not be confused with being kind or helpful to them individually. Streisand presents a classic case of a limousine liberal bleeding for the downtrodden in general while outrageously mistreating the help.

The Hollywood grapevine is filled with stories about how horrible Barbra can be to those who work for her. Once on Barbra's birthday, her cook, Bing Fong, prepared a cake. But by the time the party started, the icing was hard. Barbra told him to "replace the frosting." Fong said it couldn't be done. Streisand's husband, Jon Peters, pushed Fong violently against the sink, causing a serious injury. When Fong filed a lawsuit, Streisand and Peters settled the case out of court.

Journalists have picked up on how her staff and employees quake in their boots when she is around, waiting for an eruption of abuse. They can see the nervousness and concern in their eyes whenever she is around.[7]

Brad Meltzer worked for Streisand for a year and a half and left on good terms. "She was generous in terms of large amounts—big charities, things like that," he said, "but absolutely mean and niggardly about the salaries of the working people she hired. I recall once that Jon [Peters] had hired some young Mexican workers who had no green cards and paid them three-fifty an hour, but the work wasn't getting done fast enough. Barbra wanted them to work overtime. They asked for an additional twenty-five cents an hour overtime. She told me to fire them and have them replaced. It killed me, but I did it." In another instance, Meltzer had to fire "an older domestic couple who had been with her since she first came to Hollywood. They seemed to have outlasted their usefulness. She gave me orders that the couple had to be out by Saturday of that same week," before Barbra returned from a trip.[8]

Streisand gives speeches about the need for a higher "working wage," but some of her own employees would be glad to get any wage. After the gardener went unpaid for several months, he went to the Streisand home to complain. There was a confrontation and he left after a revolver was pointed at him. Over the years, pool contractors, a masonry supply company, and a general contractor, all hired to do work at her Malibu ranch, had to place liens on the property in order to get paid. Unpaid bills ranged from $4,500 to $50,000.[9] She was also sued by (and settled with) a screenwriter she had commissioned to write a script who claimed she would not pay him.[10]

On the movie set or on tour, she could be mean and abusive to the help. On the set of *Funny Girl,* she had veteran makeup lady Gertrude Wheeler literally in tears. "She doesn't go out of her way [for people]," said friend and producer William Wyler. "It's not her manner to be especially gracious. It's just not in her makeup; that's not the girl."[11]

That may be an understatement. Streisand has what the *New York Times* once called a reputation as a "full-fledged girl monster." Many of those who worked with her—Walter Matthau, Peter Bogdanovich, Kris Kristofferson—found her impossible. ("Filming with Streisand is an experience which may have cured me of the movies," Kristofferson said.)[12] Crew members are told to "look away" when she passes them lest they lose their job. They are forbidden to watch rehearsals. When she sang at the MGM Grand in Las Vegas for $10 million a performance, hotel employees who might encounter her in the hallway were under strict instructions to turn their backs to avoid eye contact.[13]

It's no crime to be abusive or intemperate in dealing with employees. Similar stories can be told of many other Hollywood stars. But it does contradict her public image as a champion of "working men and women." Somehow, however, this blatant hypocrisy never seems to catch up with her.

Publicly, Streisand considers the right to free speech and dissent one of the most important in the world. She waxes on about the sanctity of the First Amendment and contributes large sums to activist groups like the ACLU. But when she gives concerts in the United States or around the world, she insists that the musicians sign "secrecy agreements" that preclude them from saying anything about her. The rule applies not just to the press, but also to family and friends. This practice proved a bit much even for her apolitical and otherwise admiring biographer Anne Edwards, who wrote: "Her authoritarian demand of employees to sign papers that bind them to silence, to threaten the loss of their jobs if they discuss their work with her, is at extreme odds with all her professed liberalism. And although such tactics are not unconstitutional unless they emanate from a government agency, it is a gag order, an infringement on the right of the free speech of others. . . . The double standard here is both shocking and disappointing."[14]

Streisand's double standard on civil liberties goes deeper, however. She rants against the Patriot Act for "[trampling] on our civil liberties" and complains about suspected terrorists detained in Guantanamo Bay.[15] But in Streisand's world, civil liberties that apply in Gitmo may be suspended in Hollywood.

For example, in the summer of 2004, photographer Wendell Wall was taking pictures of Streisand and her husband James Brolin. Wall was a paparazzo who worked for several publications and made sixty-five thousand dollars a year snapping photos of Drew Barrymore, Leonardo DiCaprio, and others on a regular basis. He was Barbra

Streisand's neighbor and lived only a quarter of a mile away. They knew each other and Streisand had never filed a complaint against him; it had been months since he had snapped any pictures of her. On this day, Wall got a tip that Streisand and Brolin were at a car dealership and he decided to take a few pictures. (According to police records, Streisand was looking at SUVs—Land Rovers and a Jeep Grand Cherokee. Only months earlier she had pleaded in the left-wing magazine *Tikkun* that Americans needed to get serious about "[reducing] the release of fossil fuel emissions into our atmosphere" through more stringent conservation. Apparently she meant the "other" Americans—that is, Americans other than herself.)

Streisand noticed Wall after about twenty minutes, but there was no confrontation. Wall left, dropped the film off for processing, and had some lunch. Then he headed home, where much to his surprise he was greeted by sheriff's deputies who arrested him for stalking. His initial bail was jacked up to $1 million (well above the usual $150,000). Incredibly, the inoffensive photographer was held for three days, based on Streisand's claim that he represented some sort of physical threat.

When prosecutors looked into the case, however, they immediately concluded otherwise. Wall had no violent history, no earlier complaints, and there was nothing to indicate that he had done anything remotely illegal. In the end, they refused to press charges against him because there was "insufficient evidence of a credible threat of harm to the victims." Instead, what was supposedly a case of stalking quickly turned into a civil liberties issue. "He was never a stalker," said his attorney. "He's a photographic journalist. He was taking photos in public places on public property."

Wall sued the sheriff's department for violation of his civil liberties. (Curiously, the American Civil Liberties Union, which often gets involved in free speech cases involving the press, stayed out of this one. Perhaps it had something to do with the fact that Streisand is a heavy financial supporter.) Meanwhile, the sheriff's office launched an internal investigation and concluded that if the case went to trial, a jury would likely find in Wall's favor. Fearing that it could cost them more than $300,000, the cops agreed to settle out of court.[16]

Streisand's vaunted solidarity with the working masses doesn't extend very far. She may have criticized capitalists and conservatives for their "selfish individualism" and "indifference to the suffering of many."[17] She may talk about the necessity of labor unions to protect a "living wage." But Streisand herself has always been the consummate capitalist. She has been making her own films for twenty years and owns several production companies, the most successful of which is called Barwood Films. And like her fellow economic populist Michael Moore, she prefers to do her filming and postproduction work in Canada, where she can pay less than American union wages and get healthy tax breaks from the Canadian government.

The Long Island Incident dealt with the tragic shootings on a commuter train outside of New York City; Streisand filmed it in Toronto. *Serving in Silence,* about a lesbian in the American military, was shot in Vancouver. She did the same with *Frankie and Hazel* (Vancouver) and *What Makes a Family* (Toronto). By doing so she paid wages about 20 to 30 percent lower than the American union scale. Barwood Films also enjoyed the film and video production services tax credit, the provincial film and television production services tax credit, and a federal tax shelter program. Next time the Los Angeles Labor Council organizes one of its protests concerning the outsourcing of film industry jobs to Canada, it's unlikely Barbra Streisand will be invited to speak.

"Greed" is a label that Streisand likes to attach to the American business community and capitalists in general. But when Streisand herself needs money to support her extravagant lifestyle, avarice is suddenly acceptable. In 1993, after years of lavish spending and little work, she discovered she was almost broke. As she admitted to the *Washington Post,* she started "running out of money because I don't work very often, and I bought all this land and I can't sell my other land and so I'm going to have to sing just to pay for my house."[18]

The best way to bring in money quickly was to organize a concert tour. It had been twenty-seven years since she last appeared onstage, and interest was expected to be high. So promotion began for an international tour, and sticker shock emerged when the ticket prices were posted. Front row seats could set you back $1,000 apiece, far higher than anything anyone had ever been asked to pay. In Australia, where tickets were $930 (Australian), the *Sydney Morning Herald* dubbed her Barbra "People Who Love Money" Streisand.[19] In all, Streisand was projected to make $10 million a night. Some loyal fans wanted to see her so badly, they mortgaged their homes. "I actually took a loan against my house to get my tickets for Streisand's first concert," one fan said. "It was worth every penny I spent, and I spent a small fortune."[20] The outrageous prices were justified on the grounds that this was absolutely the last time Barbra Streisand would ever sing in public. But she pulled the same stunt seven years later, when she staged a series of high-priced "millennium" concerts.

Streisand has said that, unlike Republicans, she doesn't want to "cater to the rich. I'd rather pay more taxes."[21] Such talk comes easily to wealthy liberals like Streisand. But when it comes to her own money, she is shrewd—sometimes too shrewd. When she tried to sell her Malibu property in the early 1990s, she put it on the market for $16 million. When she couldn't find a buyer, she hiked the price to $19 million. Then she dropped the price to $11.9 million. Finally she donated the property to the Santa Monica Mountains Conservancy and took a $15 million write-off.

How could she claim a $15 million deduction for a house that wouldn't sell for $11.9 million? That's what the IRS wanted to know. Streisand entered into private negotiations with the IRS and resolved the matter quietly.[22]

More than any other issue in recent years, Streisand has been animated by the environmentalist cause. She established a Streisand Chair on Global Climatic Change at the Environmental Defense Fund and gives heavily to environmentalist causes. Her message has been downright alarmist. "I find the shrinking of the ozone layer and melting icecaps frightening," she told a Democratic Congressional Campaign Gala shortly before she went shopping for a new SUV.[23] "We can continue to thrive on this earth, but in order to do so, we must adapt to a more sustainable way of life," she wrote in *Tikkun* magazine. "While there is still some time to alter our way of living, we must begin now to behave respectfully and honor these sacred gifts—our rolling hills and mountains, the depths of our blue oceans and rivers, the richness of our forests and plants and the vastness of our land." She is particularly concerned about "the release of fossil fuel emissions into our atmosphere" and by overconsumption of our natural resources.[24]

Strong words, particularly from someone who consumed so much water to keep her Malibu lawn green that the annual bill was twenty-two thousand dollars. Or who diverted a freshwater stream on her property and had it moved a hundred yards so she could have a nicer lawn.[25] And the property she donated to a conservation group for a tax write-off? It came with serious septic tank problems that had never been fixed. (Sewage was leaking into the groundwater.)

Nor would Streisand let her ardent environmentalism get in the way of a good tax deduction. A few years back she bought a large share in the Home-Stake Production Company, described by federal officials as a "Tulsa oil drilling and tax shelter operation."[26]

When an electricity shortage gripped the state of California in June 2001, Barbra helpfully advised people to not use their air conditioners so much and dry their clothes outside. But when her spokesman was asked if Barbra was going to do the same, the spokesman shot back: "You really expect me to ask her that?" It turns out that Streisand is an air-conditioning addict. As one friend told reporters, "She is someone who cannot be hot, not even for a second."[27]

Conspicuous consumption is a problem that applies to other people, not Streisand. Her current residence (for two people) features five separate homes and a twelve-thousand-foot air conditioned barn that she uses to store her show business and music artifacts. Another residence that she recently sold in the Holmby Hills section of Beverly Hills featured a parking garage for ten vehicles. As Pat Conroy, who lived in one of her homes when he converted his best-selling novel into the movie *Prince of Tides,* put it: "She lives like Marie Antoinette."[28]

Barbra may sincerely believe that depletion and overuse of fossil fuels are a threat to the environment—but she evidently doesn't think that such concerns should get in the way of a good investment opportunity. In addition to the tax shelter mentioned above, Streisand seems to have a particular taste for investing in oil companies. Over the last several years, Streisand's foundation has held tens of thousands of dollars of stock in Williams Companies (oil and natural gas pipelines), Schlumberger, and Patterson Energy (oil drilling), Nabors Industries (offshore oil drilling platforms), British Petroleum, Kinder Morgan Inc. (another oil pipeline company), and El Paso Corporation (coal mining). There is not one solar energy or hydrogen fuel-cell developer in the lot. Like fellow antiwar hypocrite Michael Moore, she has also owned shares in Halliburton, and while she may have problems with American militarism, the military-industrial complex still pays well. Thus she has held shares in Honeywell and Lockheed Martin, two large defense contractors.[29]

Streisand is hardly ignorant of these investments. To the contrary, she has bragged to *Fortune* magazine that she is an astute stock-picker. Moreover, along with her political left hand Margaret Tabankin, Streisand is the only board member of her foundation.

The California Coastal Records Project is the brain-child of dot-com millionaires Ken and Gabrielle Adelman. These two environmentalists proudly live the life that they espouse. Their home is powered by the largest residential solar energy system in California and they own four electric cars. Their goal in establishing the Records Project in 2002 was simple: to take photos of the entire California coastline and post the pictures online. Already environmentalists have used the photos to stop the construction of illegal seawalls. The only part of the 1,150-mile coastline they decided not to shoot was near Vandenberg Air Force Base, due to fears that the photos might be used by terrorists. Otherwise they had never encountered any problems—until they ran into Barbra Streisand.

As with every one of the other twelve thousand photos they had taken, the Adelmans flew over water and snapped photos of Streisand's enormous Point Dume estate, with its half dozen homes and six chimneys, then posted them on the Internet. Streisand demanded that the photos be taken down, claiming that they violated her privacy and property rights. The Adelmans refused, saying that they were simply trying to document coastal erosion in the area.

Streisand promptly sued them for $50 million, but the Adelmans refused to back down. To the contrary, they claimed that Streisand was then "in the process of doing extensive development on her blufftop estate" and was less concerned with her privacy rights than with preventing documentation of "numerous violations" of development regulations. Environmentalists were outraged. "It is inconceivable to me that someone who proclaims herself an environmentalist would threaten to dismantle one of the greatest high-tech projects to protect the California coast in all time just because they chose to place their backyard on a coastal bluff," said Mark Massara of the Sierra Club's Coastal Program. "At some point, someone needs to sit down and tell her the public interest is at stake here."

Give the Sierra Club credit. They were the only environmentalist group to which Streisand gives money that came out against her on this issue.

The case went to trial, and Los Angeles Superior Court Judge Allan Goodman dismissed the lawsuit on the grounds that Streisand was violating the Adelmans' "free speech rights on a matter of public concern." (Again, the ACLU was conspicuously silent about a case that involved one of its major donors.) For good measure, the judge ordered Streisand to pay the Adelmans' legal bills.

Streisand not only prides herself on being an environmentalist, she also considers herself a champion for racial minorities who have been historically oppressed and who she believes continue to suffer from persistent racism. She claims common cause with blacks because as a Jew, she too has faced oppression. "With a shared history of oppression and slavery, as well as a common ingrained culture of social justice, blacks and Jews, over the years and still today, have been natural allies."[30]

Perhaps her closest political ally is Jesse Jackson. "I'm a sucker for Jesse," she declared with what can only be called unconscious irony at the Fourth Annual Awards Dinner of the Rainbow/PUSH Coalition in 2001. "Jesse represents meaning to me because he doesn't duck the hard case. Against segregation in the South. Against racial profiling in the North. Against apartheid in South Africa." She speaks about the need to open the "locked doors" of racism and has been a strong supporter of affirmative action. She also considers many of the policies that Republicans advocate to be racist.[31] Over the years she has given large sums of money to the Alliance for Justice and Operation Rainbow/PUSH Coalition.

But don't let Streisand's friendship with Jackson fool you. All her talk about racism and affirmative action shouldn't be taken to mean that Streisand actually wants to hire blacks herself.

Streisand employs a large number of people through her various production companies. I examined the credits for her films and videos, particularly those that she produces. (I purposely excluded her earliest pictures, when she was just a performer and didn't make hiring decisions.) In keeping with the practice of other liberal hypocrites like Michael Moore and Al Franken, it's hard to find a single case where she has hired a black employee in a senior position. In fact, out of sixty-three producers and directors she has hired for various projects since 1983, only one was black. (For the record, it was Whoopi Goldberg, who costarred in her picture *What Makes a Family*. Goldberg apparently insists on a producer credit for all of her pictures.) Even when Streisand produced a film on an explicitly black subject—the documentary *City at Peace*, about gang violence in Washington, D.C.—she hired white producers and a white director.

When she is not fighting environmental dangers or institutionalized racism, Streisand can be counted on as one of the consummate foot soldiers in the feminist war against patriarchy. Her commitment to feminist activism goes back over thirty years. Her movie *Up the Sandbox* is regarded as one of the first feminist films. She also endowed a chair in Women's Studies at the University of California.

Streisand has tirelessly sounded the theme of female oppression in her many speeches and interviews. She has told women around the country that they live in an oppressive patriarchy and speculates on its roots in masculine dependence and jealousy. "Fear is behind the need to subjugate. Is it because men resent us for making babies? Is it jealousy because we can give birth? . . . Does dependency create resentment? A female births a man, she gives life to a man."[32] Female empowerment in her view is not only just but vital to the future of the country, the planet, and even the galaxy: "We as women have a responsibility to put our energy and talent into repairing the universe."[33]

But does Streisand really live in fear of patriarchy? Not really. In fact, in one of her more candid moments, she revealed that she actually likes it. "I'm a feminist, but I know my secret thoughts. There are certain things that I enjoy. Women come with fathers, or dreams of fathers, being taken care of and protected, even though my feminist side says people should be independent and not need to be taken care of by another person, that doesn't necessarily work that way. There's the human factor, you know." She went on to explain that she likes "strong men" who will "protect her."[34] All three of her husbands—Elliott Gould, Jon Peters, and James Brolin—are strong male personalities. Her longtime business manager is a man, and she has by and large had most of her business affairs conducted by men. Her feminist cry may be that women must "repair the universe," but she'll leave it to men to care for her, protect her, and watch out for her interests.

Fund-raiser, friend of presidents, informal adviser to congressional leaders, Barbra Streisand has transcended her role as an entertainer and become a force in American politics. As one of the most effective political fund-raisers in America, Streisand will continue to be a major force in the Democratic Party and an important voice in political affairs, even if few outside her circle of admirers and friends take her all that seriously.

Like the conservatives she denounces, Streisand hires the best people to manage her affairs and produce her films—not those who conform to some affirmative action quota system or utopian feminist agenda. She invests wisely, like a consummate capitalist, whether she wants to admit it or not. And when she feels that her privacy or business interests might be threatened, she is prepared to protect herself with every means at her disposal. In short, much of Streisand's personal and professional success comes from the fact that she does not listen to her own advice.

GLORIA STEINEM

Hopeless Romantic, Dependent Female, Serial Monogamist

It was sunrise on an early-September morning in Stillwater, Oklahoma, and a small assembly had gathered for a wedding. The bride was in white and the groom held her hand. A friend read the wedding vows in both English and Cherokee, and a local judge watched to make it all official. The air smelled like cedar smoke. . . .

If Bella Abzug and Betty Friedan were the militants of the feminist movement, Gloria Steinem was the wonder girl. Just as committed to the cause as her sisters in arms, it was Steinem who made feminism glamorous, fun, and chic. More than any other figure in the movement, she brought feminism into the mainstream and led millions to embrace her philosophy of life, relationships, and society at large. She has lectured on thousands of college campuses, sold millions of books, and influenced two generations of American women.

She first made a name for herself by going "undercover" as a *Playboy* bunny at one of Hugh Hefner's clubs and exposing sexism in the *Playboy* empire. (One wonders what else she expected to find.) She helped launch the National Women's Political Caucus and then *Ms.* magazine, the first feminist glossy intended for a wide audience. Steinem set as her goal the remaking of the American family and transforming gender roles. She wrote dozens of articles on everything from politics to menstrual cycles. Some of it was quite funny, including one article speculating on what would happen if men had menstrual cycles. (Her conclusion: They would brag about whose was the longest and most painful.) But much of her writing was direct and uncompromising. Through her articles and the media attention her magazine garnered, Steinem became a national sensation, named woman of the year by *McCall's* and considered presidential material by some of her fans.

The magazine's founders said they wanted a collectivist approach that would be different from male-controlled publications that were too "hierarchical." Steinem, who had worked in the magazine business, criticized other publications for their lack of "democracy." But when corporate titan Warner Communications jumped in with $1 million in capital, Steinem and a handful of investors took control of all the stock.[1] The magazine lasted until 1979, when it folded under a wave of red ink. According to the *Columbia Journalism Review,* part of the problem was caused by the magazine's writers, "who successfully dodged deadlines by shamelessly deferring to their unique victim status."[2]

The magazine has since been resurrected, killed, and resurrected again. But Steinem has never looked back. Through a string of best-selling books and an intense schedule of lectures on college campuses, she remains America's most influential, eloquent, and revered feminist. One British paper accurately calls her the field marshal of feminism, the Wellington of womanism.

Steinem's message has always been about more than abortion, pay equity, and sexual harassment. Beyond her advocacy for certain laws, she has always paraded herself as a guide for women on how to navigate difficult questions about men, marriage, family, and societal norms. But she has rarely followed her own advice—and her life is all the better because of it.

Some of the contradictions between the Steinem message and reality are skin-deep, literally. For decades she has railed against what she regards as the cult of beauty: the fact that women are judged by their appearance rather than their intellect. Society's valuation of women by their looks, she says, makes them "commodities" and robs them of their autonomy and humanity. As she recently told students at the University of Missouri, it is wrong and antifeminist to "stress looks."[3]

But Steinem herself has always been about glamour and beauty. What brought her to the forefront of the movement and put her head and shoulders above contemporaries like Bella Abzug was her stylish looks. And her beauty was something that she worked on and was always very conscious of. Before she appeared on the *Today* show at age fifty-two, she had an operation to remove excess fat from her eyelids. When asked about it later, she explained that the procedure was not done because she was getting older or because she intended to change her appearance. It was simply a "self-esteem" question. (Though if stressing looks is antifeminist, how and why would this enhance her self-esteem?) Pressed further, she admitted that she would not have had the surgery if she were not going to appear on *Today*.[4]

Steinem could be forgiven a contradiction between what she says and what she does if it were limited to this small act of vanity. But she has a well-established pattern of encouraging other women to repress their desires on certain fundamental questions, only to act on those desires herself. And her other hypocrisies are far deeper and more damaging to those who have heeded her advice.

Nowhere is that more true or profound than when it comes to relationships with men. As a feminist, Steinem has always promoted the view that men are an appendage and that independence and autonomy are desirable feminist goals. She popularized the phrase (coined by a fellow feminist), "A woman needs a man like a fish needs a bicycle." When it comes to matters of the heart, she has always proclaimed herself an advocate of relationships with men that are enjoyable, sexually satisfying, and intellectually stimulating, but has rejected traditional notions such as romance and marriage. One of her more famous articles for *Ms.* was called "Why I Will Never Marry."

Romance, for example, according to Steinem is simply a tool of patriarchal domination. In her international bestseller *Revolution from Within: A Book of Self-Esteem* (it reached #1 in the United States and was translated into eleven languages), she told women that "the more patriarchal and gender-polarized a culture is, the more addicted to romance." Romance prevents the discovery of your own unique self, she wrote. It entraps you and prevents you from realizing your feminist goals. "The truth is that finding ourselves brings more excitement and well-being than anything romance has to offer, and somewhere, we know that."[5] Sexual relations with men are there to enjoy, she writes, but don't let romance destroy your autonomy. Instead, women should embrace feminism and then "become the men we wanted to marry" by meeting their own financial and emotional needs.[6]

Romance with a man means abandoning the feminist cause; it is a distraction from more important goals. "Romance itself serves a larger political purpose by offering at least a temporary reward for gender roles and threatening rebels with loneliness and rejection." Obviously Steinem has thought a lot about this. "[Romance] also minimizes the very anti-patriarchal and revolutionary possibility that women and men will realize each other's shared humanity when we are together physically for the sexual and procreative purposes society needs." Romance, in short, is a political and personal dead end and any truly committed feminist should have nothing to do with it. "The Roman 'bread and circuses' way of keeping the masses happy—and the French saying that 'marriage is the only adventure open to the middle class'—might now be updated. The circus of romance distracts us with what is, from society's point of view, a safe adventure." Romance "privatizes our hopes and distracts us from making societal changes." Romance is a selfish and frivolous act, she tells women, something to be avoided at all costs because it is a myth that will ultimately lead to disappointment, jealousy, and finally violence. She even denounces teenage girls who dot their i's with little hearts in letters to their boyfriends.

But while Steinem was writing those words, encouraging young women to turn their backs on long-term romantic relationships with men, she herself was engaged in a longtime relationship with television writer, producer, and musician Blair Chotzinoff. The two had met in college and almost married until Steinem called it off. But over the next three decades they kept the relationship going. They went to cozy restaurants, drank wine, and shared quiet moments together. When he visited New York, they would walk together arm in arm. When asked about the relationship in 1998, Steinem had no hesitation in describing it as a long-term romance, "And romance," she explained, "is about passion and curiosity, things we both share."[7]

Steinem also carried on a three-year relationship with New York real estate magnate and publisher Mort Zuckerman. Zuckerman would seem to be everything that Steinem was against: a type-A male and prominent conservative who lavished expensive gifts on her. After they broke up, she again—without a trace of irony—categorized their relationship as "a romance."[8]

If Steinem has advised women to avoid romance lest they stray from the feminist path, she has been downright hostile about the institution of marriage. Reading through her books, speeches, and newspaper articles since 1977, I couldn't find a single positive word about it.

In her book *Outrageous Acts and Everyday Rebellions,* she explains that marriage is really an "ownership contract" that oppresses women and prevents them from being who they should be.[9] She has told students on college campuses around the country that "marriage is designed for a person and a half," She wrote on another occasion, "For the sake of those who wish to live in equal partnership, we have to abolish and reform the institution of marriage." In 1987 she exclaimed that when a woman marries, she becomes a "semi-non-person." She once told the League of Women Voters that being a married woman is like being a part-time prostitute.

"I can't mate in captivity," she would say to appreciative laughter. "Marriage is like a vacuum cleaner," she advised her friends. "If you stick it to your ear, it sucks out all your talent." Steinem told her friend Marlo Thomas that she rejected marriage, as a symbol that she had "conquered . . . our middle class values."[10] In 1995, Steinem told one interviewer, "I can't imagine why I would get legally married." She explained that in marriage there is "loss of identity," and that in "traditional marriage, dependency may have looked like love, but it sure didn't feel like love."[11] In a 1999 interview, she rejected the "traditional feminine" notion that you should have "a man in your life."[12]

Then Steinem met David Bale, at (of all places) an abortion rights rally. The South African multimillionaire, with a beautiful home in Malibu, had made his money importing skateboards and blue jeans into Great Britain. (As with almost all of Steinem's relationships, she was attracted to a wealthy, successful, highly driven man.) Steinem continued to speak on college campuses urging young women to avoid the pitfalls of romance and marriage. But in September 2000, while attending a Native American festival in Stillwater, Oklahoma, the lovers decided to tie the knot. The vows were administered by the appropriately named Wilma Mankiller, a longtime friend and former chief of the Cherokee Nation. Afterward, Steinem released a statement saying that she was pleased to "take advantage" of the opportunity to marry. "I hope this proves what feminists have always said—that feminism is about the ability to choose what's right at each time of our lives."

But, of course, this was untrue. Steinem had never advocated marriage as a healthy choice. Just two years earlier, in 1998, she had advised students at the University of Pennsylvania to avoid marriage because of terrible laws and destructive societal values.[13] After her marriage, however, she suddenly announced that everything had changed, explaining that marriage laws had finally been made equitable: "Now the laws are different. It is possible now to make an equal marriage."[14] She never explained how so much progress had been made in two short years. As one British newspaper put it, if a woman needs a man like a fish needs a bicycle, Steinem was now riding in the Tour de France.[15]

Before she met Bale, she had told millions of American women that marriage is an "inauthentic choice" and that married women were sacrificing their "autonomy." Now she and her husband were talking about estate planning and filing joint tax returns.[16] (Tragically, Bale died two years later.)

Steinem might have viewed her marriage to Bale as a personal choice appropriate to her time of life, but to feminists who had considered her an ally and exemplar, the news was quite a shock. "It's just wonderful that she's found romance and economic security," deadpanned the feminist author Susan Brownmiller. "I'm just speculating, but those are the reasons you get married. Right?"[17]

Younger feminists on college campuses, who were expecting to follow in her footsteps, saw even more clearly the hypocrisy in Steinem's belated embrace of marriage. Gina Hamadey wrote in the *Michigan Daily News* that she was "selfishly disappointed" by the act because she considered Steinem a major influence on her life. "Why couldn't they have been lifelong partners like Susan Sarandon and Tim Robbins? Why did she need that ring on her finger after breaking off an engagement in college and speaking out against it ever since?"[18]

Steinem's response to such criticism made no mention of feminist autonomy. "Why do it instead of just living together? For us, we wanted a way of saying that we were committed to each other. If we'd been younger, perhaps we would have had a child or done something else to say that we are committed together."[19]

Nor was this the first time that Steinem had contemplated marriage, in direct contradiction of her publicly stated philosophy. During the 1970s she had taken out not one but two marriage licenses with screenwriter Robert Benton. In the end, she never went through with it; but she never let on to her followers that she was flirting with an institution that she had made a career of condemning. And when she was dating Mort Zuckerman, friends recall her visiting fertility clinics to explore the possibility of having children with the real estate mogul.

Nor is Steinem alone among radical feminists. Many others of that pioneering generation discovered sooner or later that they needed the comforts of marriage and traditional gender roles. As Sally Quinn wrote in the *Washington Post*, "The 'feminists,' and by that I mean the people who spoke for the movement, were never completely honest with women. They didn't tell the truth. They were hypocritical."

In Steinem's case, that hypocrisy is particularly cruel. For Steinem, the glamorous poster-girl of feminist autonomy, marriage was always an option, available at a moment's notice. She never lacked for suitors. Many of the women who listened to her, who rejected marriage and romance to show their commitment to the cause, never really had that option. As feminist Nicci Gerrard wrote after the wedding, "Feminists of the Sixties and Seventies have had to pay a terrible price for their dedication—most of them now are forgotten, reviled, poor and alone."[20]

Steinem has never recanted her views about marriage, romance, and relationships with men, even though she has embraced the very choices that over the course of her career she condemned. But in the end, by rejecting her own advice, she has made her life richer and more rewarding. All one can say is, better late than never.

▶▶ *CORNEL WEST*

Segregationist, Commodity Fetishist, Capitalist Interest-Maximizer

Cornel West has been called a mesmerizing preacher, a black Jeremiah, and the most gifted black thinker in American history. Hyperbole aside, he is a sharp-talking, quick-thinking professor who writes best-selling books and is one of the most popular speakers on college campuses today. On almost any day of the week you can find him in front of an audience expounding to thousands of students on a wide range of topics. He has dined with President Clinton and advised political figures from Bill Bradley to Al Sharpton and Louis Farrakhan. You might see him on the news standing next to millionaire rapper Sean Combs (P. Diddy) or doing a cameo appearance in the latest *Matrix* sequel. And in just about every venue, you will find him inveighing with great indignation against the prevalence of "white supremacy" in America and the predatory evils of capitalism.

West was born in 1953 in Oklahoma but raised in Sacramento, California. His father was a contractor for the U.S. military and his mother was a teacher. West describes his childhood as a period of enlightenment about how viciously racist America is. Yet racism does not seem to have affected his family directly. His mother was the only black teacher in an all-white school and later became a popular principal. (In 2001 an elementary school in Sacramento was named for her.) While her son rages against "white supremacy" and paints a bleak picture of his upbringing, recalling incidents of racism at the community swimming pool, his mother doesn't recall any racial conflict. "The kids and parents were just wonderful," she told the *Sacramento Bee* in 1999. "I never encountered any racial prejudice."[1]

As a teenager in the 1960s, young Cornel fell under the spell of the Black Panthers. His family attended church near a local Panther office and soon he was spending time there, absorbing their radical views and their negative vision of America. "As a youth," he has written, "I resonated with the sincere black militancy of Malcolm X, the defiant rage of the Black Panther Party."[2] He got the chance to prove his revolutionary bona fides when his pregnant teacher asked the class to say the Pledge of Allegiance. West refused. When she forced him, West punched her in the face and was expelled from school. "He was very violent as a young kid," recalls his brother Clifton.[3]

In 1970, West enrolled at Harvard University, among the first generation of blacks to be admitted to the college in significant numbers. West was by all accounts a committed and serious student. He majored in philosophy but changed to Near Eastern Languages and Literature so he could graduate a year early. Along the way he managed to participate in the takeover and occupation of the Harvard president's office in 1972. He then went on to Princeton for a PhD. He has since taught at Princeton, Harvard, and is now again at Princeton.

But though he has been rewarded many times over by the "racist" American system, his hatred for America has apparently never diminished. When terrorists attacked on September 11, West emerged on the Harvard campus to explain that the terrible event represented the "niggerization of America" and would serve a useful purpose if whites could finally understand what it meant to be black. On another occasion he told students, in all seriousness, "America is really a chamber of horrors."[4]

West is also a proud Marxist and has remained committed to Marxism even in the face of its manifest failures. Indeed, after the collapse of the Soviet Union in 1989, he paradoxically declared that "Marxist thought becomes even more relevant after the collapse of communism in the Soviet Union and Eastern Europe than it was before."[5] Time and again he has written that to understand racism, poverty, and world affairs in general, Marxist analysis is the only proper lens.

West is profoundly hostile to capitalism, which he regards as evil in both spirit and practice, telling students on one campus that "unregulated, unfettered capitalism is *killing us.*"[6] According to West, we need to wage implacable war against "unaccountable corporate power with its obscene levels of wealth and inequality."[7] It is hard to find a single example of his finding anything positive to say about capitalism or the free market. "It's so difficult to live a human and humane life under a market-driven civilization," he told students on one occasion.[8] Of course, as a tenured professor, West is sheltered from the harsh market forces he denounces, and from which he indirectly benefits.

A self-described revolutionary, West warns that without socialism, "we are simply headed toward Armageddon. I mean race war. . . . That's quite imaginable in this society."[9] Moreover, blacks who try to escape urban poverty by starting their own business or otherwise striving upward are condemned as race traitors and sellouts. As a founding member of the Black Radical Congress, West unequivocally rejects "Black capitalism."[10] With the fire and brimstone of a preacher, he attacks middle-class blacks who are "preoccupied with getting over—with acquiring pleasure, property and power."[11] West despises middle-class blacks who have embraced the "culture of consumption" and want to send their kids to Ivy League colleges so they can "get a better job (for direct selfish reasons)."[12] He scolds them for pursuing the "American Dream," which he defines as "conspicuous consumption and hedonistic indulgence."[13] His advice to students is to avoid the temptation to make money altogether. He warns that "the world waiting for you with all of its seductions, its hollowness, its shallowness," springs from an evil capitalist impulse.[14]

For West, socialist revolution is the only morally serious response to these conditions. Here he is equally critical of other leaders on the left whom he believes are too comfortable with the capitalist system. He wondered aloud at one conference how many were prepared to die for the cause: "That's a major challenge, especially given the privileged status of so many leftists these days. Let's talk about that—who's willing to die under what conditions? I mean, that's what the Communists were talking about in the 30s, that's what I love about the Reds in the 30s, they were willing to die."[15]

Yet despite his calls for revolution, his condemnation of capitalism, and his denunciation of blacks who aspire to wealth and comfort, West is himself the consummate entrepreneurial capitalist. With an appetite for expensive cars, thousand-dollar suits, and million-dollar homes, the question isn't whether he's willing to die for the cause, but whether he is willing to take a meager pay cut.

As a professor of religion and director of Afro-American Studies at Princeton University in 1993, Cornel West had written a couple of obscure books about philosophy that didn't get much notice. Even so, the Marxist critic was famous for cruising around town in his "plush Cadillac Sedan de Ville."[16] West's taste for the finer things was not lost on his colleagues. Professor Gerald Early of Washington University, another noted black writer and intellectual, remarked that while West tried his best to "conceal his bourgeois ambition," everyone in the field was aware of it.[17]

It was with the publication of his book *Race Matters* in 1993 that he was suddenly able to unleash his acquisitive impulses. Sitting near the top of the *New York Times* best-seller list in the months following the L.A. riots, *Race Matters* made West a national star. He was featured in *Newsweek* and *Time* magazines and hit the lecture circuit like a force of nature. Delivering five lectures a week, he insisted on receiving fifteen thousand dollars a shot. Professor Henry Louis Gates of Harvard, head of the Afro-American Studies Department, was constantly on the phone trying to lure him to teach at Cambridge. West was coy, telling the *Daily Princetonian* that he could never live in Boston; it lacked the necessary black culture to make him feel at home. But quietly the negotiations continued as the president of Princeton offered him a salary increase and two additional assistants. Boston didn't experience an influx of black culture over the next two months, but Harvard did up its offer to close to three hundred thousand dollars. Suddenly West, who had criticized other blacks for "market calculation,"[18] was on his way to Cambridge.

At Harvard, West was the beneficiary of corporate largesse and support. He might decry "multinational corporate capitalism" and "corporate influence" in higher education,[19] but that didn't prevent him from enjoying its benefits. His salary at Harvard (among the highest on campus) came from his post as the Alphonse Fletcher, Jr., University Professor of Afro-American Studies, which was funded with a $3 million donation from one of the shrewdest stock-pickers on Wall Street, Alphonse "Buddy" Fletcher. The department's beautiful brick building overlooking Harvard Yard came courtesy of corporate grants from companies like Time Warner. By 2001 the department had sixteen faculty members and only fifty-five declared majors. Projects done for corporate sponsors made up the difference, such as the effort to distribute African-American literature through McDonald's during Black

History Month. (Ironically, West has criticized what he calls the "McDonaldization of the World.") West was also paid for work by companies like HBO, Ernst & Young, and Warner Music. Microsoft came along with a lucrative grant to develop an African-American history database.

Meanwhile, West remained active on the lecture circuit, his exorbitant fee forcing many colleges to charge admission ($29 at UC-Davis) to hear him expound on the evils of capitalism.[20] He was paid that amount to give a speech at Haverford College, where he upbraided students for their desire to become wealthy and powerful. In his "own humble opinion," he said, one of the "major forms of idolatry of our day" is "the market way of life."[21]

Then there was the "Conversation on Race" held on Martha's Vineyard. (During the mike check, West said, "One-two-three Farrakhan Farrakhan.") For $50 a ticket, the public got to hear West lecture about the evils of capitalism and the "income disparities" that were hurting America. When asked whether it made sense to hold such a conference on Martha's Vineyard, Gates replied, "This is a very middle-class place."[22]

West's mounting wealth afforded him the opportunity to plunge heavily into the Boston real estate market. Publicly he criticized middle-class blacks for their greed and materialism. Privately, this socialist paragon revealed his true colors when he bought homes in two of Boston's best neighborhoods. According to real estate records, he bought a condominium valued at $820,000 on Boylston Street, while his primary home on Commonwealth Avenue in Newton cost him more than a million. (These are not quite Noam Chomsky numbers, but West is a good twenty years younger, so he has plenty of time to catch up.) Naturally, the Wests also hired a maid.

West has repeatedly lambasted other upwardly mobile blacks for abandoning the inner city and moving into white neighborhoods. America is a place of "chocolate cities and vanilla suburbs," he says, and in *Race Matters* he called middle-class blacks "decadent" for abandoning their "brothers and sisters" and fleeing to the suburbs and their "shopping malls.[23] For those who may be wondering about West's flavor of choice, the black population in Newton is only 2 percent.[24]

West taught a wildly popular Introduction to African-American Studies course that attracted hundreds of students a year. The class counted as a core requirement in history, and by all accounts West gave quite a moving performance. His lectures were not a dull recitation of academic theories but were often compared to a Baptist revival meeting. (The popularity of the course may also have had something to do with the fact that approximately 90 percent of the students received A's.) West would draw upon what he called "funkadelic" beats and music from the Supremes for inspiration. West's course "isn't a class, it's like attending church on a Sunday morning," said Harvard student Amma Y. Ghartey-Tagoe. "I was sitting in the front row going 'mm-hmmmm' and 'amen' to everything Professor West was saying."[25]

West also continued to churn out books. He wrote very little that was actually new or original, but instead reprinted articles and included excerpts from his interviews and texts of his speeches. This practice dismayed even supporters and fans, like the student newspaper, *The*

Harvard Crimson. As the paper noted in an editorial about *The Future of Race,* a book West "co-authored" with Du Bois Professor Henry Louis Gates Jr., "a good portion of this $21 book is simply reprinted essays." The *Crimson* concluded that marketing it "with a title that is both deceptive and weighty for a book that is half reprinted essays, is an example of using words like 'race' to sell books."[26]

He next decided that he wanted to go into the music business. After all, that's where the real money is. West went around to various record companies looking for offers. When none were to his liking, he decided to form his own company. Along with his brother Clifton, an old school friend named Mike Dailey, and rap producer Derek "D.O.A." Allen, West set up Four Black Men Who Mean Business, Inc. to produce and market an album called *Sketches of My life.* With a heavy beat in the background, West extemporaneously spit out lyrics on racism, the evils of capitalism, and racial pride.

> *From the heights of rich African humanity,*
> *to the depth of sick American barbarity,*
> *in the whirlwinds of white supremacy,*
> *black people preserved their sanity and dignity*
> *. . . No other people in the modern world have had*
>   *such unprecedented levels of unregulated violence*
>   *against them.*

West was obviously pleased with the result. As he wrote on his web site, cornelwest.com: "In all modesty this project constitutes a watershed moment in musical history. The combination of the oratorical passion and unmatched eloquence of Dr. Cornel West with the particular musical genius of Derek 'D.O.A.' Allen has produced an auditory theatrical experience." For good measure, West described himself as "one of the most preeminent minds of our time."

When the Institute of Politics at Harvard invited him to give a speech shortly after completing the album, he showed up, played some tracks from his CD, and offered them to the students for twenty-five dollars apiece. He repeated the same performance on other campuses: Instead of delivering a lecture, he would play a few songs before hawking copies of his CD to the audience.[27]

The CD sold a modest 1,040 copies in the first two months and went downhill from there. Traditional rappers were unimpressed. ("We think he looks like Gene Shalit," said *Ego Trip*, a hip-hop mag.) Undeterred, West and his company engaged in an aggressive marketing campaign to get the CD distributed as part of a Black History Month promotion and sought out a series of "licensing agreements with African-American organizations."[28] No capitalist exploiter could have done better.

Two years later, West released yet another CD entitled *Street Knowledge*. This time he tried to land a deal with a larger label, but when there were again no takers, he went to little-known Roc Entertainment. West claims that his CDs are not about commercial exploitation or making money. He calls them examples of "danceable education."[29]

But not everyone was pleased with West's "pedagogic" exercise. Harvard's new president, Lawrence Summers, viewed West's numerous extracurricular activities as a distraction from his primary mission of teaching and research. (In addition to promoting the CD, West was advising Al Sharpton on his presidential bid.)

In September 2001, Summers called West into his office to discuss his work, as he had done with every other academic department. West reportedly left the meeting upset because he had been "disrespected" by Summers. But he said nothing publicly about it.

Meanwhile, Princeton University had been in quiet negotiations with West for almost a year about the prospects of his returning there. No doubt West, as a highly sought after academic, had asked for favorable terms. As Cynthia Garcia Coll, chairman of Brown University's education department, put it, because of the relatively small number of African-American scholars, "a culture of competition" for them exists at top-flight universities. "When you get to be at the level of Professor West, you sort of feel like a commodity."[30] Still, one can only imagine what sort of demands would lead negotiations for a faculty position to take an entire year.

Notwithstanding his talk about the evils of capitalism and the marketplace, not to mention his advice for young people to reject material concerns, West played out the drama like a first-rate sports agent. Two months after his meeting with Summers, as his negotiations with Princeton continued, West suddenly went public and described with a great show of indignation how offended he had been by Summers's comments. "I have never been attacked and insulted in that particular way," he said. He not only excoriated Summers for suggesting that he focus more on research and writing than on producing rap albums, but complained that Harvard's president had not bothered to visit him in the hospital during his recent prostate surgery. The *New York Times* and other media outlets picked up on the story, and it quickly became a test case for "racism" on college campuses.

Summers was quite surprised by West's reaction and quickly asked for another meeting, hoping to persuade him to stay and promising to "compete vigorously to make this an attractive environment" for him. West now had two major universities publicly competing for his services.

In early January, West and Summers met again. Princeton had made an offer, but apparently it was not good enough. This time, word leaked out that the meeting with Summers had gone well. Afro-American Studies Department head Henry Louis Gates said everything was patched up: "As far as I'm concerned the issue is resolved."[31]

But the issue was far from resolved. With the encouragement of West and his friends, a petition drive was launched to encourage him to stay. The Black Students Association collected twelve hundred signatures from faculty and students asking him not to go. Meanwhile, negotiations continued with Princeton. Finally a deal was struck, and West announced that he was leaving Harvard. "I am excited to return to the greatest center for humanistic studies in the country," West said.

The decision came as a complete surprise to the Harvard Black Students Association, which had rallied to his side and collected all those signatures. According to association members, West never even contacted them to say "thank you" before he left.[32] The *Harvard Crimson,* which had been strongly supportive of West, called it "a childish departure . . . West's recent antics have made him look patently ridiculous. Rather than exiting gracefully and showing a suitable degree of class, he has acted like a spoiled child."[33]

Actually, the *Crimson* missed the point. West only appeared to be acting like a spoiled child. In fact, he had acted like an academic free agent making skillful use of the media and campus resources in order to leverage his value in the marketplace.

Since returning to Princeton, West has continued to exploit his celebrity status in exchange for capitalist gain. In 2003 he hit the road with a couple of prominent friends, author Michael Eric Dyson and radio host Tavis Smiley, for a "Pass the Mic! Tour." For fifty dollars a ticket, blacks were encouraged to come and hear the three of them discuss the issues of the day. West talked about "capital accumulation" as a social ill. During a recent speech at the University of North Carolina–Pembroke, he complained that people were pursuing "material toys" and railed about the "corrupting culture of wealth."[34] Meanwhile, he moved into another nice neighborhood (in suburban New Jersey), this one with just over a 5 percent black population.

Throughout his peregrinations from one Ivy League school to another, West has been repeatedly asked whether he would ever consider teaching at a historically black college like Howard, Morehouse, or Spelman. Both on C-SPAN and to a conference of black academics his answer was a quick "no." The reason? West casually explains that those institutions could never afford his six-figure salary.[35] Yet in his best-seller *Race Matters,* West goes out of his way to criticize black parents who no longer send their children to black colleges like Howard and Morehouse but instead try to get their kids into the Ivy League "to get a high-paying job." West considered this an act of "selfishness."

Cornel West loves to give a good sermon, exhorting students to abandon their interest in money and pursue the cause of socialist transformation. It is time, he has said, to "bridge the gap between one's rhetoric and reality, one's promise and performance."[36] Yet West is a success today precisely because he has learned to exploit the market for his services in good capitalist fashion. Perhaps he should heed his own advice, or at least quit giving it to others.

▶▶ CONCLUSION
The End of Liberal Hypocrisy

Conservatives who abandon their principles and engage in hypocrisy usually end up harming themselves and their families. But as we have seen, liberals who do the same usually benefit.

How can we explain the fact that so many prominent individuals who are so passionate about their beliefs don't act accordingly? That seems to be the great paradox of liberalism as practiced by those we have profiled. They are deeply committed to certain values and beliefs, but rather than embrace these ideas and live by them in the small universe they control, they instead focus on faraway or abstract matters. And who can blame them? It's a lot more satisfying to call someone else a racist than to actually practice affirmative action yourself, with all the trouble that entails. In short, they seem more interested in compelling others to embrace their vision of social change than in acting on that vision themselves.

Al Franken, Michael Moore, and Barbra Streisand are not racists because they hire few (or no) blacks. They are simply hiring the most qualified individuals available at that particular time for the job. Nancy Pelosi doesn't despise working people just because she eschews labor unions in the businesses that her family owns. She is simply trying to run those businesses efficiently and effectively. Ted Kennedy doesn't care less about the environment because he's in the oil business. He sees a business opportunity that is profitable and takes advantage of it. Hillary Clinton, Kennedy, Soros, Streisand, and the others are not greedy and selfish simply because they try to avoid paying more in taxes. They (or in the Kennedys' case, their forebears) worked hard for their wealth and are trying to preserve it for their children. Gloria Steinem is not anti-woman just because she got married. She fell in love and found someone she wanted to spend the rest of her life with. All these individuals are simply making private decisions that are in their own best interest.

The real question is not why they live the way they do, but why they continue to espouse ideas that so baldly contradict their behavior. Why can't they stop affixing sinister labels—racist, greedy, polluter—to people who are doing the exact same thing they are, only without hypocrisy?

Ignorance is not the reason. All of these individuals profess to take ideas seriously and seem to have given considerable thought to what they believe. We are not talking about light-headed actresses who spout trendy slogans because they want to be with the Hollywood "in" crowd.

All of the people profiled here closely follow events, read political works, discuss them seriously, and passionately embrace a liberal/left worldview. So lack of information is not the problem.

The answer, I fear, is more sinister. Experience has taught these individuals that their ideas just don't work. When it comes to the fundamentals—the things that matter most in their lives—they suddenly forget about affirmative action, environmentalism, progressive taxation, and antiglobalist hostility. They really don't respect their own ideas and have privately concluded, whether they admit it to themselves or not, that liberalism as practiced today does not offer them a road map to happiness. *Soak the rich,* but don't soak me. *Protect the environment,* but let me drive my Hummer and water my lawn. *Workers of the world, unite!* But running a business with a union shop is just too complicated and difficult. *Hire more blacks to fight racism,* but let me hire my own people based on ability, not race. *Romance and marriage are a form of patriarchal oppression,* but I still want wine and roses and a powerful man to sweep me off my feet.

The simple fact is that those in the vanguard of the liberal-left have found their own ideas to be ultimately self-defeating, self-destructive, and unworkable.

So why do they continue to cling to them? Clearly these slogans still offer a potent weapon with which they can cudgel their enemies. Charges of racism and greed, for example, still carry some currency in America, particularly in certain communities. Sometimes the label will stick. Even if it doesn't, the targets will spend quite some time backpedaling or explaining themselves. Either way, such charges are a useful weapon when it comes to political combat.

But the real tragedy is that many people see these ideas as being more than a weapon. Even if the people we have profiled here don't live by the ideas they espouse, *millions of other people are trying to do so.* Noam Chomsky may prudently pack away money and set up a trust in order to avoid paying taxes, but students on college campuses who take him at his word are making life decisions that will lead them to avoid acquiring any sort of wealth in a well-meaning attempt to live up to his exalted standards. In short, they will live a life more consistent with Chomsky's ideas than Chomsky lives himself . . . and they will suffer for it. Michael Moore may play the stock market like a pro, but millions of others who heed his advice to stay out are going to be less well off in retirement. Cornel West may be a consummate exploiter of the academic employment market, but young black students who admire his "solidarity" with the black working class may turn their backs on a business career in an attempt to remain morally clean. Gloria Steinem may have tied the knot in middle age. But what do we say to the thousands of women who heeded her advice all those years to eschew romance and marriage?

These liberal/left leaders live in a near-perfect world because no one has held them accountable. The mainstream media is certainly not on their case. They can enjoy the moral satisfaction that comes with the knowledge that they, unlike the rest of us, are committed to fighting racism, oppression, inequality, and pollution—in short, that they are more concerned and idealistic than the rest of us. But this idealism and concern doesn't cost them anything, because they and their families continue to reap the benefits that come from living like conservatives.

It is time for the free ride to end. Next time any of the individuals profiled in this book happens to appear on a college campus or pontificates on cable television about a moral or political issue, the first question you should ask is. Sure . . . but do you really live your life that way?

▶▶ notes

INTRODUCTION

1. Patricia DiLucchi, "Dr. Laura How Could You?" *Salon*, November 3, 1998.
2. Quoted in Adam Smith, "Castor Strives to Dispel Doubts in Senate Quest," *St. Petersburg Times*, April 12, 2004.
3. Transcript, *The Chris Matthews Show, Weekend*, November 7–8, 2004.
4. James Lakely, "Dean Defends Imitation of Rush," *Washington Times*, May 23, 2005.
5. Allan Colmes, *Red, White & Liberal: How the Left Is Right and the Right Is Wrong* (New York: Regan Books, 2003).
6. Courtney Leatherman, "Gloria Watkins: The Real bell hooks," *Chronicle of Higher Education*, May 19, 1995.
7. "The Racial Breakdown of Congressional Staffs," *National Journal*, June 21, 2005.
8. *U.S. Supreme Court United States v. Wells Fargo Bank*, 485 U.S. 351 (1988), and *United States v. Wells Fargo Bank et al.*, Appeal from the United States District Court for

the Central District of California No. 86–1521 (Wells Fargo was the executor of the Jules Stein estate).

9.   Michael Specter, "The Dangerous Philosopher," *New Yorker,* September 6, 1999.

10. See Jeff Sharlet, "Why Are We Afraid of Peter Singer?" *Chronicle of Higher Education,* March 10, 2000.

11. Peter Berkowitz, "Other People's Mothers," *New Republic,* January 10, 2000.

NOAM CHOMSKY

1.   Maya Jaggi, "Conscience of a Nation," *The Guardian,* January 20, 2001.

2.   Quoted in Peter Collier and David Horowitz, *The Anti-Chomsky Reader* (San Francisco: Encounter Books, 2004).

3.   Pinker cited a psychologist named Jonathan Haidt, who studies "moral awe," the feeling inspired by a king or a Mother Teresa. According to Haidt, an understated appearance offers proof of moral nobility. "I don't think it's by design," Pinker told the *New Yorker,* "but I think the fact that Chomsky is so unflashy adds to the feeling of awe that people come away with." Larissa MacFarquhar, "The Devil's Accountant," *New Yorker,* March 31, 2003.

4.   Noam Chomsky, *Power and Terror* (Seven Stories Press, 2003), p. 80.

5.   Jonathan Curiel, "MIT Linguist Critiques U.S. Foreign Policy," *San Francisco Chronicle,* March 18, 2002.

6.   Jacklyn Martin, "Is Chomsky 'Anti-American'? " *The Herald,* December 9, 2002.

7.   Richard Todd, "The 'Ins' and 'Outs' at MIT," *New York Times,* May 18, 1969.

8. Israel Shenker, "A Linguistics Expert Who Believes That Academicians Should Also Be Activists," *New York Times*, October 27, 1968.

9. "An Urgent Invitation to Faculty Members," *The Tech*, May 6, 1969.

10. During the Vietnam War, he sat on the advisory board of the Greater Boston High School Student Mobilization Committee, which worked aggressively to halt ROTC programs on college campuses and high schools in the Boston area. See "School Students against Vietnam War," *Bay State Banner*, June 29, 1967, p. 3. During the first Gulf War in 1991, he advocated protest actions against ROTC and "campus military centers." Noam Chomsky, "Gulf War Pullout," *Z* magazine, February 1991.

11. Bert F. Green, *Digital Computers in Research: An Introduction for Behaviorial and Social Scientists* (McGraw-Hill, 1963).

12. This background research on linguistics and the military comes from Chris Knight, "Noam Chomsky; Politics or Science?" *What Next? Marxist Discussion Journal* 26 (2003): pp. 1–29.

13. Robert W. McChesney, introduction to Chomsky's *Profit over People* (Seven Stories Press, 1998), p. 11.

14. Robert F. Barsky, *Noam Chomsky: A Life of Dissent* (Cambridge: MIT Press, 1997), p. 215.

15. For an example of his class-warfare "us versus them" formula, see Bill Frezza, "A Lion in Winter," *The Tech* [MIT student newspaper], February 20, 2004.

16. Howard Zinn, *The Future of History* (Common Courage Press, 1999), p. 55; and throughout his memoir *You Can't Be Neutral on a Moving Train* (Beacon Press, 2002).

17. Jay Parini, "Noam Is an Island," *Mother Jones*, October 1988, p. 39.

18. See the interview with Noam Chomsky, "Marginalizing the Masses," *Journal of International Affairs,* spring 2000; and Noam Chomsky, "Domestic Constituencies," *Z* magazine, May 1998.

19. Noam Chomsky, *Class Warfare* (Common Courage Press, 1996), p. 256.

20. *Harvard Educational Review.*

21. Information on the law firm comes from http://www. palmerdodge.com/dspSingleBio.cfm?BioID=987. Among the books assigned to the trust include his book on linguistics, *New Horizons in the Study of Language,* published by the Cambridge University Press in numerous editions, as well as some editions of *Powers and Prospects.* It is unknown what other assets he has assigned to the trust.

22. John Lloyd, "Blessed Are the Pure in Heart," *New Statesman,* April 23, 2001.

23. Noam Chomsky in *Talking about a Revolution* (South End Press, 1998), p. 24.

24. "Strong Foreign Sales for Chomsky," *Publishers Weekly,* December 3, 2001.

25. "Globalization and Its Discontents," Noam Chomsky debates with *Washington Post* readers, available on chomsky.info

26. http://www.chomsky.info/copyright.html

27. Comments from Chomsky on "Globalization and Its Discontents with Noam Chomsky," Washington Post .com forum, May 16, 2000.

28. Deborah Bolling, "Noam Way," *Philadelphia City Paper,* October 10–16, 2002.

29. In 2002, Chomsky cosigned a letter stating, "We recently learned that through our retirement funds invested in TIAA-CREF that we have been made inadvertent supporters" of the government in Burma.

The letter refers to the fact that TIAA-CREF owned shares in the oil giant Unocal, which had investments in that country. The TIAA-CREF fund in question was the stock fund.

30. Chomsky, *Class Warfare*, p. 186.
31. Ibid., p. 62.
32. Parini, "Noam Is an Island," p. 39.
33. Noam Chomsky, speech delivered on April 13, 1970, in Hanoi while visiting North Vietnam with antiwar activists. The speech was broadcast by Radio Hanoi on April 14 and published in the *Asia-Pacific Daily Report*, Foreign Broadcast Information Service, April 16, 1970, pp. K2–K3.
34. See Noam Chomsky, *For Reasons of State* (Pantheon 1973), pp. 230–32.
35. M. H. Lagarde, "Cuba Always Has Been with Him," *La Jiribila* [Cuba], no. 129.
36. Ibid.; and Joaquin Rivery Tur and Aldo Madruga, "Chomsky Condemns U.S. World Domination Strategy," *Granma*, October 29, 2003.
37. "Interview with Noam Chomsky at CLACSO Conference," Radio Havana, October 28, 2003.
38. Muralidhar Reddy, "The Response in Pakistan," *Frontline* (India), December 8–21, 2001.
39. Ibid.

MICHAEL MOORE

1. Liz Braun, "Moore's a Blue-Collar Gadfly," *Toronto Sun*, April 8, 1998.
2. Ibid.
3. Larissa MacFarquhar, "The Populist," *New Yorker*, February 16 and 23, 2004.

4. Ibid.; Braun, "Moore's a Blue-Collar Gadfly."

5. Jon Ronson, "The Egos Have Landed," *Sight and Sound,* November 2002.

6. Shawn Windsor, "The Many Roles of Michael Moore," *Detroit Free Press,* February 28, 2004.

7. Deborah Schoenemann and Benjamin Nugent, "Intelligencer," *New York,* February 2, 2004.

8. "Briefly ... Hypocrisy, Moore Style," *Winchester Star* (Virginia) , October 31, 2003.

9. Geoff Olson, "What Keeps Michael Moore Going?" *Common Ground,* December 2003.

10. Cindy Fuchs, "Up to His Old Tricks," *Philadelphia City Paper,* April 9–16, 2003.

11. Michael Moore, interview with Bill Maher, "Fear Factor," at the WGA.org web site.

12. Steven Zeitchik, "Michael Moore: The New JFK?" *Publisher's Weekly,* October 27, 2003; and MacFarquhar, "The Populist."

13. Samantha Ellis, "*Fahrenheit 911* Gets Help Offer from Hezbollah," *The Guardian,* June 17, 2004.

14. "The German Cult of Michael Moore," *Deutsche Welle,* October 25, 2003.

15. Ibid.

16. Quotes from Louis B. Hobson, "Bowling for Hollers," *Calgary Sun,* August 17, 2003; and David Brooks, "All Hail Moore," *New York Times,* June 26, 2004.

17. Michael Moore, *Stupid White Men* (New York: Warner Books, 2003), p. 57.

18. Ibid., p. 67.

19. Michael Moore, interview in *Tikkun,* November–December 1998.

20. I used the authoritative database imdb.com to determine film credits.

21. Moore, *Stupid White Men*, p. 54.
22. Michael Moore, *Dude, Where's My Country?* (New York: Warner Books, 2003), pp. 116, 137.
23. Moore, *Stupid White Men*, pp. 16–17, 238; MacFarquhar, "The Populist."
24. Moore, *Stupid White Men*, p. xvi.
25. See Michael Moore's letter at http://www.salon.com/july97/moore970703.html
26. Michael Moore, *Booknotes* interview, November 16, 2003.
27. See the PF990 forms Michael Moore filed for his Center for Alternative Media and Culture.
28. Elaine Dutka, "New Michael Moore Project Gives Drug Companies a Sick Feeling," *Detroit News*, December 22, 2004.
29. Director's chair interview, industrycentral.net
30. Michael Moore, interview with Brian Lamb on *Booknotes*, November 16, 2003.
31. MacFarquhar, "The Populist."
32. Daniel Lyons, "Harvey and Me," *Forbes*, September 6, 2004.
33. Michael Moore, *Downsize This* (New York: Perennial, 1997).
34. Quoted in Vance Lehmkuhl, "Michael Moore: Twenty Questions," *Philadelphia City Paper*, September 5–12, 1996.
35. MacFarquhar, "The Populist."
36. John Pierson, *Spike, Mike, Slackers, and Dykes* (Miramax Books), p. 175.
37. Kathleen Antrins, "Moore Now Getting Less," *San Francisco Examiner*, February 28, 2005.

1. "Franken Sense: Transformed from Comic to Cult Critic, Twin Cities Native Al Franken Has Found His Niche as the Loudest Mouth on the Left," *Minneapolis Star-Tribune,* October 18, 2003.

2. Russell Shorto, "Al Franken, Seriously So," *New York Times Magazine,* March 21, 2004.

3. Ibid.

4. Bruce Alpert, "Conservative Christians Pray Bush Takes Cue," *Times-Picayune* (New Orleans), January 24, 2005.

5. Weston Kosova, "Live from the Left, It's . . . " *Newsweek,* March 29, 2004.

6. Al Franken, *Rush Limbaugh Is a Big Fat Idiot,* (New York: Dell, 1999) p. 72.

7. Al Franken, *Lies and the Lying Liars Who Tell Them: A Fair and Balanced Look at the Right* (New York: Dutton, 2003), p. 139.

8. Comments on CNN, March 28, 2004, Vanderbilt Television News Archive.

9. Shorto, "Al Franken."

10. Al Franken interview with Richard Blow, *Mother Jones,* November–December 1996.

11. "Press Needs to Work a Little Harder," *USA Today,* August 30, 2004.

12. Franken, *Lies,* p. xi.

13. Graydon Royce, "Al Franken Roils Political Waters and More," *Minneapolis Star-Tribune,* November 28, 2000.

14. "Franken Sense."

15. Franken, *Rush Limbaugh,* p. 216.

16. "Flouting Conventions," *People,* June 20, 1992.

17. Richard S. Lee, "Live from New York: It's Al Franken," *Harvard Crimson,* April 16, 1976.

18. Anne K. Kofol, "Oh the Things He Knows," *Harvard Crimson,* June 5, 2002.

19. William G. Clotworthy, *Saturday Night Live: Equal Opportunity Offender* (1st Books, 2001). Clotworthy was a censor for *SNL.*

20. Ibid.

21. Doug Hill and Jeff Weingrad, *Saturday Night: A Backstage History of Saturday Night Live* (New York: William Morrow, 1986), p. 238.

22. Ibid., p. 333.

23. Richard Goldstein, "Shtick and Soul," *Village Voice,* March 23, 1999.

24. "Cowboys vs. Steelers," *Washington Times,* January 28, 1996.

25. Christopher Andersen, *Bill and Hillary: The Marriage* (Best Sellers, 1999).

26. National Press Club Luncheon with Al Franken, Comedian and Author, National Press Club, February 28, 2002.

27. Franken, *Lies,* p. 85.

28. This division of Franken's lies comes from Ned Rice, a writer for HBO's *Real Time with Bill Maher,* in *Human Events,* September 22, 2003.

29. Shorto, "Al Franken."

30. Franken, *Lies.*

31. Hana R. Alberts, "Al Franken Talks 'Lies,'" *Harvard Crimson,* October 3, 2003; Franken, *Lies,* p. xii.

32. Max Cleland, *Strong at the Broken Places* (Longstreet Press, 2000).

33. These instances of Franken errors were first brought to my attention by the web site Frankenlies.com. I have independently verified them.

34. Franken's son attended the Dalton School in Manhattan.

35. Alberts, "Al Franken Talks 'Lies.'"

36. Franken, *Lies,* p. 253.

37. Ibid., p. 258.

38. Ibid., pp. 257, 259.

39. Ibid., p. 258.

40. Teja Arboleda, *In the Shadow of Race: Growing Up as a Multi-ethnic, Multicultural, and 'Multiracial' American* (Lawrence Erlbaum Associates, 1998), p. 215.

TED KENNEDY

1. "Kennedy Divides Merchandise Mart," *Chicago Tribune,* March 22, 1947.

2. Michael C. Jensen, "Managing the Kennedy Millions," *New York Times,* June 12, 1977.

3. See his U.S. Senate personal finance disclosures.

4. "Kennedy Family Trust Said to Be Undertaxed on Chicago Properties," *New York Times,* May 15, 1980.

5. Richard Burgess, "Retired Judge Set to Settle with IRS," *The Advertiser* (Lafayette, Louisiana), March 31, 2004.

6. My original article for *National Review*; and Andrew Miga, "Ted K and Kin Landed Sweet Deal: Minority-Owner Rules Waived for Purchase of D.C. Parcel," *Boston Herald,* October 18, 1994.

7. Tara Cassidy, "Soviet, American Politicians Stress Need for Unity at UMASS Gathering," *Boston Globe,* April 22, 1990.

8. Stephanie Ebbert, "Kennedy Opposes Wind Farm," *Boston Globe,* August 8, 2003.

9. Ian Fein, "Wind Farm Project Clears Key Hurdle," *Martha's Vineyard Gazette,* November 12, 2004; and John Leaning, "Draft Report Favorable to Wind Farm," *Cape Cod Times,* November 8, 2004.

10. No. 89–CA–1114, Supreme Court of Mississippi, 622 So. 2d 291; 1993 Miss. LEXIS 317; 126 Oil & Gas Rep. 509, August 12, 1993, Decided.

11. George Lardner Jr., "... and an Oil-Rich Presidential Dynasty," *Washington Post,* December 9, 1979.

12. For the ins and outs of royalty trusts, see Richard Lehmann, "Northern Exposure," *Forbes,* September 6, 2004, p. 206,

13. "Heavily Armed Kennedy Guard Is Arrested," *San Jose Mercury News,* January 14, 1986.

14. Cassidy, "Soviet, American Politicians Stress Need for Unity."

HILLARY CLINTON

1. "First Lady Urges Grads to 'Right the Balance' of Responsibility," *Lexington Herald-Leader* (Kentucky), May 2, 1993.

2. Martha Sherrill, "Hillary Clinton's Inner Politics," *Washington Post,* May 6, 1993.

3. Martin E. Marty, "Methodist in Deed," *Christian Century,* November 16, 1994.

4. Angie Cannon and Frank Greve, "Hillary Clinton Invested $1,000, Netted $100,000 Through Trading," *Seattle Times,* March 30, 1994; David Savage, "GOP Uses Whitewater to Tie Clinton to 'Decade of Greed,' " *Los Angeles Times,* August 14, 1995; Alexis Moore, "Clinton: He Wants to Renew Communal Responsibility for Our Progress, Work, Integrity, Service, Family," *Miami Herald,* March 8, 1992; James Risen, "Whitewater Affair Raises the Spectre of Hypocrisy for Clintons," *Los Angeles Times,* May 1, 1994.

5. Carl Cannon, "Clintons' Middle-Class Image Fades, Figures Show Life of Prosperity," *The Record* (New Jersey), March 27, 1994; and Dave Shiflett, "The First Lady's Shameful Secret," *Rocky Mountain News,* April 4, 1994.

6. Maureen Dowd, "Your Fault, No, Yours, No, Yours," *New York Times,* February 21, 2001.

7. See, for example, George Lardner Jr., "Clinton Shipped Furniture Year Ago," *Washington Post,* February 10, 2001.

8. Robert Holland, "Virginians Need No Moral Instruction from Clinton and Taxes and Schools," *Richmond Times-Dispatch,* November 12, 1997.

9. "Money Audits the Clintons," *Money,* April 1994.

10. Committee Reports, 104th Congress, Senate Report 104–280. Investigation of Whitewater Development Corporation and Related Matters, June 17, 1996.

11. Don Feder, "Yuppie Greed in Whitewater," *Boston Herald,* March 21, 1994.

12. Lisa Daigle, "Estate Tax Repeal a Bipartisan Effort," *American Banker,* February 1, 2001.

13. Hillary Clinton, *Living History* (Simon & Schuster), p. 109.

14. Ibid., p. 110.

15. Quoted in Zelda Bronstein, et al., "Feminist Pundits and Hillary Clinton," *Dissent,* summer 1997.

16. Midge Decter, "The Little Woman of Little Rock," *Commentary,* May 1994.

17. Melanie Cooper, Thomas M. DeFrank, Peter Goldman, Tom Matthews, Mark Miller, Andrew Murr, Patrick Rogers, *Quest for the Presidency* (Texas A&M University Press, 1992), p. 638.

18. Charles Krauthammer, "The Real Crime of Whitewater Is the Hypocrisy of Bill and Hillary Clinton," *Pittsburgh Post-Gazette,* January 15, 1996.

19. Roger Morris, *Partners in Power: The Clintons and Their America* (New York: Henry Holt, 1996), p. 449.

20. "Lafarge Copee: Affiliated Firms Are Fined for Arranging Price-Fixing," *Wall Street Journal*, December 27, 1991; and "Lafarge Corporation: Slowdown, Strike Contribute to 87% Decline in Earnings," *Wall Street Journal*, July 19, 1991.

21. Charles Babcock, "The Clintons' Finances: A Reflection of Their State's Power Structure," *Washington Post*, July 21, 1992.

22. Ibid.

23. David Maranis, *First in His Class: A Biography of Bill Clinton* (New York: Simon & Schuster, 1996).

24. *Business Week*, April 18, 1992.

25. Greg Anrig and Elizabeth MacDonald, "How Hillary Manages the Clintons' Money," *Money*, July 1992.

26. Stephen A. Smith, "Compromise, Consensus, Consistency," in Ernest Dumas, *The Clintons of Arkansas* (Fayetteville: University of Arkansas Press, 1993).

27. Quoted in Maureen Dowd, "First Lady Becomes a Contradiction," *New York Times*, August 10, 1995.

28. See Howard Schneider and Susan Schmidt, "Whitewater Repossessions Sales Practice Benefited Clintons, Partners," *Washington Post*, April 21, 1994; and Charles Babock and Susan Schmidt, "Records Show Wider Role for Hillary Clinton Whitewater Papers Detail Involvement," *Washington Post*, April 13, 1994.

29. Schneider and Schmidt, "Whitewater Repossessions"; Morris, *Partners in Power*, p. 377; and Risen, "Whitewater Affair."

30. See, for example, her comments and introduction of the legislation for the Predatory Lending Consumer Protection Act of 2003.

31. Christopher Lasch, "Hillary Clinton, Child Saver," *Harper's,* October 1992.

32. Garry Wills, "H. R. Clinton's Case," *New York Review of Books,* March 5, 1992; and Michael Barone, "Taking Hillary Seriously," syndicated column, July 8, 1999.

33. Matthew Cooper et al., "The Hillary Factor," *U.S. News and World Report,* April 27, 1992.

34. Glenn Blain, "Abortion May Be Pivotal in NY Race," *Westchester County News,* August 28, 2000.

35. Susan Schindehette et al., "The Ties That Bind," *People,* February 15, 1999.

36. "Clintons Share Discipline, Setting Rules for Chelsea," Associated Press, August 24, 1993; and Greg McDonald, "It's Hard to Be Young: Schoolkids Pour Out Hearts in an Exchange with Clinton," *Houston Chronicle,* February 21, 1993.

37. Quote is from Neel Lattimore, spokeswoman for Hillary Clinton in "Chelsea Clinton Turns 'Sweet 16,' Parents Put Brake on Gift of a Car," *Buffalo News,* February 28, 1996.

38. Gregg Zoroya, "Sweet Sixteen: Chelsea Clinton Is Growing Up . . . " *Los Angeles Times,* February 28, 1996.

39. "Clintons Pick Ritzy School for Daughter," *The Pantagraph* (Bloomington, Illinois), January 6, 1993.

40. Aleta Payne, "School Vouchers: Having It Both Ways," *San Jose Mercury News,* September 20, 1993.

41. Quoted in Don Feder, "Will Say Anything to Keep Teachers' Union Happy," *Human Events,* February 18, 2000.

42. "Wyden Urges Clinton to Send Daughter to Public School," *The Oregonian,* November 22, 1992.

43. "Taking Care of Chelsea," *The News and Observer,* January 7, 1993.

44.	Donald Rothberg, "Clintons Careful in Parenting Political Life Has Brought Challenges to First Mom and Dad," *Charleston Daily Mail,* June 2, 1997.

RALPH NADER

1.	Jonathan Rowe, "Ralph Nader Reconsidered," *Washington Monthly,* February 1989, p. 65.
2.	Barbara Gamarekian, "Bringing Up Ralph Nader: A Mother's Food for Thought," *New York Times,* June 27, 1977.
3.	Charles McCarry, *Citizen Nader* (New York: Saturday Review Press, 1972), p. 62.
4.	Peter Brimelow and Leslie Spencer, "Ralph Nader, Inc.," *Forbes,* September 17, 1990.
5.	McCarry, *Citizen Nader,* p. 135.
6.	Quotes are from Nader's introduction to Charles Derber, *Corporation Nation: How Corporations Are Taking Over Our Lives and What We Can Do about It* (New York: St. Martins, 1998), pp. ix, x; Ralph Nader et al., *The Big Boys* (New York: Pantheon, 1986), p. 505; and Ralph Nader, "Overcoming the Oligarchy," *The Progressive,* January 1999.
7.	Ralph Nader, quoted in David Sanford, *Me and Ralph: Is Nader Unsafe for America?* (Washington, D.C.: New Republic Books, 1976), p. 21; and Ralph Nader et al., *Taming the Corporate Giant* (New York: W. W. Norton, 1976), pp. 132, 136.
8.	Nader, *Taming the Corporate Giant,* p. 132.
9.	Quoted in "12,000 Gather to See Nader at Fleetcenter," *Harvard Crimson,* October 2, 2000.
10.	Brimelow and Spencer, "Ralph Nader, Inc."
11.	See Dan M. Burt, *Abuse of Trust: A Report on Ralph Nader's Network* (Chicago: Regnery, 1982).

12. Brimelow and Spencer, "Ralph Nader, Inc."

13. Nader, *Big Boys*, p. 507.

14. See, for example, Ralph Nader, "Buying Rights," *Mother Earth News*, February 2000.

15. Jake Tapper, "Inside Nader's Stock Portfolio," *Salon*, October 28, 2000.

16. Matt Welch, "Nader Defends Stock-Market Loot," workingforchange.org, November 4, 2000.

17. Tapper, "Inside Nader's Stock Portfolio."

18. Declan McCullagh, "Verizon's Copyright Campaign," CNET News, August 27, 2002.

19. Sanford, *Me and Ralph*, pp. 14–15.

20. Burt, *Abuse of Trust*, p. 88.

21. This information comes from PSRI's 990 Form filed with the IRS, 1974. This trade is first mentioned in Burt, *Abuse of Trust*.

22. See the 990s filed by Nader's organization.

23. Nader, *Big Boys*, p. 507.

24. Peter Perl, "Editor Claims Firing by Nader Based on Unionization Attempt," *Washington Post*, June 28, 1984.

25. Sanford, *Me and Ralph*.

26. Nader, *Taming the Corporate Giant*, p. 19.

NANCY PELOSI

1. Quoted in Michael Crowley, "Follow the Leader," *New Republic*, November 25, 2002.

2. Joe Feuerherd, "Roots in Faith, Family, and Party Guide Pelosi's Move to Power," *National Catholic Reporter*, January 24, 2003.

3. John Nichols, "Is This the New Face of the Democratic Party?" *The Nation*, August 6, 2001.

4. Crowley, "Follow the Leader."

5. Carolyn Lochlead, "Helms Ejects House Women from Hearing," *San Francisco Chronicle*, October 28, 1999.

6. Danny Dolinger, "Banner Hangers Face Five to Life: Oil Mongers Settle for 10 Grand," *Earth First!* December 31, 1998.

7. The best newspaper account of the CordeValle saga comes from a series of columns by Barry Witt of the *San Jose Mercury News*. Witt was apparently unaware of the Pelosis' involvement with the project. See his columns in the *News* on June 24, 2003, June 12, 2003, June 5, 2003, May 8, 2003, April 24, 2003, March 13, 2003, and February 20, 2003.

8. Barry Witt, "What to Do on CordeValle; Open It Up to Public, or Open Up Its Wallet," *San Jose Mercury News*, August 7, 2003.

9. Staff Report, Planning Commission, June 5, 2003, File: 5950-68-28-94P (CordeValle Golf Club), Lions Gate Limited Partnership, Revocation, Modification, or Reaffirmation of a Use Permit Granted for a Public Access Golf Course.

10. See File: 5950-68-28-94P, Lions Gate Limited Partnership (CordeValle Golf Club) Staff Report, San Jose Planning Commission, August 5, 2004, and the staff report with the same file number on November 4, 2004.

11. Greeting from House Democratic Leader Nancy Pelosi upon receiving the Environmental Leadership Award from Bluewater Network, September 10, 2004.

12. *Wall Street Journal,* July 16, 2004, p. A12.

13. Resolution Authorizing the Execution of a Lease between the County of San Mateo and Borel Estate Company, a California Limited Partnership, for Suite 405 of the Building at 1700 South El Camino Real, San Mateo (Lease No. 1259).

14. Martin Espinoza, "Anatomy of a Sellout," *San Francisco Bay Guardian,* October 8, 1997.

15. See "Pelosi Statement on Cesar Chavez Birthday; 'Civil Rights Leader Is an Example for All Americans,' " *PR Newswire,* March 31, 2004.

16. Congressional Record—House, July 17, 1991, 137 Cong Rec H 5528.

17. Nancy Pelosi speech to the AFL-CIO Industrial Union Council, February 2, 2004.

18. Nancy Pelosi, letter sent to Mr. Mark Huntley, president, San Francisco Multi-Employer Group, November 10, 2004.

19. Nancy Pelosi speech to the AFL-CIO Industrial Union Council, February 2, 2004.

GEORGE SOROS

1. Quoted in Miriam Hill, "George Soros: The Sound of One Billionaire Lashing," *Philadelphia Inquirer,* April 9, 2002.

2. See George Soros interview in *The Observer,* May 6, 2001; and Rachel Ehrenfeld and Shawn Macomber, "George Soros: The 'God' Who Carries Around Some Dangerous Demons," *Los Angeles Times,* October 4, 2004.

3. Michael Lewis, "The Speculator," *New Republic,* January 10, 1994–January 17, 1994.

4. Joshua Muravchik, "The Mind of George Soros," *Commentary,* March 2004.

5. George Soros, *The Crisis of Global Capitalism* (New York: Public Affairs, 1998), p. xvii.

6. Ibid., p. xxvii.

7. George Soros, *On Globalization* (New York: Public Affairs, 2002), p. 5; and Soros, *The Crisis,* p. xxviii.

8. Quoted in Brendan Murphy, "Man Who Moves Markets Also Tries to Rebuild Nations," *San Diego Tribune*, August 22, 1993.

9. "Talkative: George Soros," *The Economist*, August 7, 1993.

10. Piali Roy, "Saint George (Soros) the Drachma-Slayer," *This* magazine, July–August 2000; and Nigel Holloway, "How Contrarian," *Far Eastern Economic Review*, July 24, 1997.

11. "PM: Soros a Menace to the World," *New Straits Times*, December 22, 2002.

12. Samak Sundaravej quoted in Faisal Islam, "Rich Man, Wise Man . . . " *The Observer* (London), March 10, 2002, and "Soros: May Day Protestors Do Have a Point," *The Observer* (London), May 6, 2001.

13. Neil Clark, "The Billionaire Trader Has Become Eastern Europe's Uncrowned King and Prophet of 'The Open Society,' " *New Statesman*, June 2, 2003.

14. "World: America's Head of Brazil Bank in Soros Link," *BBC World News*, February 17, 1999.

15. "Soros Fund, President Agree to Restrictions to Settle U.S. Charges," *Wall Street Journal*, September 14, 1979.

16. "Soros Convicted of Insider Trading," *Akron Beacon Journal*, December 21, 2002.

17. Quoted in Jack Schwager, *The New Market Wizards* (Wiley, 1993).

18. Dahrendorf quoted on Australian Public Radio, "The Freedom Broker," Radio National transcripts, June 22, 1997. Skidelsky quoted in Islam, "Rich Man, Wise Man . . . "

19. George Soros, comments to Australian Public Radio, "The Freedom Broker," Radio National transcripts, June 22, 1997.

20. Paul Krugman, "Soros' Plea: Stop Me!" *Fortune*, November 23, 1998.

21. See Eric Alterman, "Target: George Soros," *The Nation,* December 29, 2003.

22. Soros, *The Crisis,* pp. 196–97; and Chrystia Freeland, "Did George Soros Really Kill the Ruble?" *New Republic,* February 8, 1999.

23. Australian Public Radio, "The Freedom Broker."

24. Mark Gimein, "George Soros Is Mad as Hell," *Fortune,* October 27, 2003.

25. Soros, *The Crisis,* p. 111.

26. Michael T. Kaufman, *Soros: The Life and Times of a Messianic Billionaire* (New York: Knopf, 2002), p. 135.

27. "Revenue Sells 600 Buildings to Bermuda-based Company," *Trends and Developments,* vol. 8, issue 10 (October 2002).

28. David Cay Johnston, "Dozens of Rich Americans Join in Fight to Retain Estate Tax," *New York Times,* February 14, 2001.

29. George Soros quoted in Kaufman, *Soros.*

30. Simon English, "The Best-Connected Investor in America," *The Telegraph,* May 27, 2003; and David Litterick, "Immarsat Chief Lined Up for 25 Million Stake," *The Telegraph,* June 10, 2003.

31. Jim Freer, "George Soros," *Latin Trade,* October 1998.

32. Gene Marcial, "A Bright Gleam on Apex," *Business Week* June 14, 2004.

33. Muravchik, "The Mind of George Soros," and Russ Baker, "George Soros's Long Strange Trip," *The Nation,* September 20, 1999.

34. George Soros in *Soros on Soros* (Wiley, 1995).

35. Baker, "George Soros' Long Strange Trip."

36. Freer, "George Soros."

37. David Horowitz and Richard Poe, "The Shadow Party," Frontpagemagazine.com

1. "Diva Democracy," *George* magazine, November 1996.
2. Liarne George, "What Would Jesus Wear?" *Maclean's,* June 21, 2004.
3. See her November 1996 interview in *George.*
4. James Spada, *Streisand: Her Life* (Ballantine, 1995), p. 288.
5. Randall Riese, *Her Name Is Barbra* (St. Martin's, 1994), p. 571.
6. Karn Carrillo, "Chavez Wants Mandela, Danny Glover to Monitor August 15 Referendum," *New York Amsterdam News,* July 22, 2004.
7. Ryan Murphy, "The Way It Is," *San Jose Mercury News,* December 24, 1991.
8. Quoted in Anne Edwards, *Streisand: A Biography* (Little Brown, 1997), p. 391.
9. Spada, *Streisand,* p. 406.
10. Riese, *Her Name Is Barbra,* p. 365.
11. Ibid., p. 285.
12. Joe Baltar, "The Way She Is," *Sacramento Bee,* December 22, 1991.
13. Liz Smith, *New York Post,* January 6, 2000.
14. Edwards, *Streisand,* pp. 496–97.
15. Barbrastreisand.com/statements.html
16. Norma Meyer, "It's Streisand vs. Paparazzo," *San Diego Union-Tribune,* January 16, 2000; and Troy Anderson, "Celebrity Photog May Get $80,000," *Daily News of Los Angeles,* October 2, 2001.
17. Jeff Jacoby, "Scrooge Doesn't Live Here," *Boston Globe,* March 29, 1994.
18. Tom Shales, "An Hour on the Coach with Barbra," *Washington Post,* December 22, 1991.
19. Owen Hughes, "High Streisand Ticket Prices Startle Concert Goers," *Billboard,* April 8, 2000.

20. Mark Brown, "Streisand: The Myth, the Music, the Moment," *Orange County Register,* February 27, 2004.

21. Jeff Simon, "Streisand, Larger Than Life," *Buffalo News,* December 8, 1991.

22. Myron Levin, "Streisand Tax Break Called into Question," *San Francisco Chronicle,* April 8, 1994.

23. Barbra Streisand speech, posted on her web site.

24. Barbra Streisand, "Stewards of the Earth," *Tikkun,* January 2000.

25. Mary McNamara, "Tourist Trap: Barbra Streisand's Donated Estate Has Been a Blessing and a Curse as a Park," *Houston Chronicle,* July 31, 2002.

26. "SEC Suit Charges Fraud to GEO Resources on Tax," *New York Times,* June 2, 1976.

27. "Streisand Accused of Hypocrisy," *The Guardian,* June 25, 2001.

28. Simon, "Streisand, Larger Than Life."

29. All this information comes from the PF990 IRS filings of the Barbra Streisand Foundation.

30. Barbra Streisand, "Let's Unite," posted on her web site, June 18, 2003.

31. Rainbow/PUSH Coalition Fourth Annual Awards Dinner, 12/11/01, posted on her web site.

32. Carrie Ricky, "A Sickness of Our Society," *Akron Beacon Journal,* December 26, 1991.

33. Riese, *Her Name Is Barbra,* p. 571.

34. Shales, "An Hour on the Coach with Barbra."

GLORIA STEINEM

1. Amy Farrell, *Yours in Sisterhood:* Ms. *Magazine and the Promise of Popular Feminism* (University of North Carolina Press, 1998), p. 40.

2. Rick Perlstein, "*Ms.* Magazine: Feminist Fighter," *Columbia Journalism Review*, November–December 2001.

3. Angela Vo, "Face of Women's Movement Doesn't Like to Stress Looks," *Missourian*, February 13, 2005.

4. Sydney Landesohn Stern, *Gloria Steinem: Her Passions, Politics, and Mystique* (Birch Lane, 1997).

5. Gloria Steinem, *Revolution from Within* (Little, Brown, 1993), p. 267.

6. Ibid., p. 263.

7. Alan Dumas, "A Love Story," *Rocky Mountain News*, June 28, 1998.

8. Stern, *Gloria Steinem*, p. 356.

9. Gloria Steinem, *Outrageous Acts and Everyday Rebellions* (New York: Henry Holt, 1995).

10. Stern, *Gloria Steinem*, p. 309.

11. Faith Popcorn, "Gloria Hallelujah!" (interview with Gloria Steinem). *Interview*, June 1995.

12. Claudia Dreifus, "Ms. Behavin' Again," *Modern Maturity*, May/June 1999.

13. Erin Johnson, "Steinem Tells U. to 'Organize for Change,'" *Daily Pennsylvanian*, November 5, 1998.

14. Lorraine Ahearn, "Gloria Steinem's Hopeful Words: Just Married," *Greensboro News & Record*, September 17, 2000; and Philip Delves Broughton, "How the Fish Found Her Bicycle," *Daily Telegraph*, July 11, 2001.

15. Broughton, "How the Fish Found Her Bicycle."

16. "A Feminist Icon Reflects on Money; Gloria Steinem Talks about the Financial Progress Women Have Made and Analyzes Her Own Strengths and Weaknesses in Managing Her Assets," *Business Week*, September 17, 2001.

17. Jennifer Frey, "Gloria Steinem Is Feminism's Unblushing Bride," *Washington Post*, September 10, 2000.

18. Gina Hamadey, "The Deflowering of Two Virgins," *Michigan Daily News,* September 21, 2000.

19. Broughton, "How the Fish Found Her Bicycle."

20. Nicci Gerrard, "Gloria in Excelsis," *The Guardian,* September 10, 2000.

CORNEL WEST

1. Fahizah Alim, "Opening Doors: Irene West Gave Her All as a Teacher and Principal, Now, a New School Honors Her Name and Hard Work," *Sacramento Bee,* June 4, 1999.

2. Cornel West, *The Cornel West Reader* (New York: Basic Books, 1999).

3. Victor A. Patton, "Why Race Still Matters," *Sacramento News and Review,* February 2, 2001.

4. Quoted in Steve Brier, "Roundtable on the Future of the Left," *Socialism and Democracy,* spring 1999.

5. Quoted in Paul Hollander, "Which God Has Failed," *New Criterion,* February 2002.

6. Denise K. Magner, "Labor Leaders and Academics Seek to Forge a New Alliance," *Chronicle of Higher Education,* October 18, 1996.

7. "West Fights for Minority Rights," *Harvard Crimson,* April 5, 2002.

8. David Kurnick, "Scholars Debate Responsibility," *Harvard Crimson,* December 1, 1992.

9. David S. Abrams, "Socialism Won't Bridge Gap," *Harvard Crimson,* April 22, 1995.

10. "Black Radical Congress: Principles of Unity," *Guild Practitioner* (Berkeley), July 31, 1998.

11. Cornel West, *Race Matters* (Beacon Press, 1993), p. 5.

12. Ibid., p. 36.

13. Ibid.

14. Miguel Navrot, "St. John's Grads Told to Be Wary," *Albuquerque Journal,* May 20, 2001.

15. Quoted in Brier, "Roundtable."

16. Robert S. Boynton, "Princeton's Public Intellectual," *New York Times,* September 15, 1991.

17. Quoted in "The Race Market," *Harvard Crimson,* May 6, 1996.

18. Nanaho Sawano, "Cornel West Opens Democracy Teach-Ins," *Harvard Crimson,* March 3, 1998.

19. "Students Hold 'Teach-Ins' to Protest Corporate Influence in Higher Education," *Chronicle of Higher Education,* March 13, 1998.

20. "Cornel West Welcomed Locally: Harvard Professor's New Album Celebrates Black Achievement; Scheduled to Speak at UC Davis," *Sacramento Observer,* April 11, 2001.

21. Quoted in Robert A. Heineman, "Ill-Conceived Calls for Public Service," *Chronicle of Higher Education,* December 7, 1994.

22. Angela Ards, "Race Matters," *Village Voice,* September 16, 1997.

23. Trish Willingham, "Speaker: Racial Woes Remain; a Harvard Professor, Who Wrote an Acclaimed Book on the Subject, Says America Is Not Solving the Problems Dividing Blacks and Whites," *The Post-Standard* (Syracuse), September 27, 1996.

24. U.S. Census 2000, Summary File 1 (SF-1), Newton, Massachusetts.

25. "Afro-Am Faces Absence of Stars," *Harvard Crimson,* February 6, 2001.

26. "The Race Market," *Harvard Crimson.*

27. Sherri Day, "A Professor Who Can Rap the Rap," *New York Times,* May 12, 2001.

28. G. Jeffrey MacDonald, "Cornel West: Professor Turned Rapper," *Christian Century,* January 2, 2002.

29. Cailey Hall, "Interview: Cornel West Gets Down to His Second CD at Campus Club," *Daily Princetonian,* May 14, 2004.

30. Zachary Goldfarb, "Relationship between Education, Race Highlighted in West Saga," *Daily Princetonian,* May 3, 2002.

31. Kate Rakoczy, "Summers, West Conflict Close to Resolution," *Harvard Crimson,* January 7, 2002.

32. Kate L. Rakoczy, "Harvard Loses West to Princeton," *Harvard Crimson,* April 12, 2002.

33. "A Childish Departure," *Harvard Crimson,* April 18, 2002.

34. Amber Rach, "West's Speech Treat for Crowd," *The Pilot,* March 16, 2005.

35. C-SPAN and Ronald A. Taylor, "Academic Theater: On the Road with Cornel West, Henry Gates, and SRO Crowds," *Black Issues in Higher Education,* May 2, 1996.

36. Joanna Weiss, "Westward Bound: Princeton Scholar Cornel R. West '74 Brings a Multi-Contextual Approach to Life and Scholarship," *Harvard Crimson,* October 30, 1992.

▶▶ *index*

"Children Under the Law" (H. Clinton), 111
Chomsky, Carol, 22
Chomsky, Noam, 16–38
  as "American dissident," 18–19, 38
  as anarchist-socialist, 19, 24
  Aspects of the Theory of Syntax by, 22
  At War with Asia by, 34
  civil violence advocated by, 23
  on class warfare, 26
  on collectivization, 35
  on corporate America, 22, 30–31, 51
  in Cuba, 35–36
  entrepreneurial success of, 19, 24, 27–29
  on free speech and independent media, 32–34, 35, 37–38
  in India, 36
  influence of, 17–18, 22, 28, 32, 152, 218
  on intellectual property rights, 29–30
  investments of, 31, 35
  on Islamic terrorism, 36–37
  La Jornada by, 35
  Manufacturing Consent by, 33
  in North Vietnam, 33–35, 36
  on personal as political, 20
  on police tactics, 36
  public appearances of, 18, 24, 27–28, 29, 30, 36
  "Responsibility of Intellectuals" by, 19–20, 23
  and September 11 attacks, 28, 36, 37
  Syntactic Structures by, 21–22
  and taxation, 23, 24, 26, 27, 30
  U.S. denounced by, 18, 33–35, 36–37
  on U.S. electoral system, 17
  and U.S. military/Pentagon, 20–24, 124
  U.S. passport of, 37
  wealth of, 24–27, 116, 207
  web site of, 29–30
  on women and minorities, 31–32
Chotzinoff, Blair, 196
Cisco Systems, 124, 130
Citizens for Tax Justice, 130
City at Peace (Streisand), 189
Clark, Neil, 161
Clark, Tom, 45–46
Cleland, Max, 71, 76
Clinton, Bill, 1, 71, 72, 201
  appetites of, 96
  good heart of, 95
  governorship of, 96, 98–99, 107–8
  and Hillary; *see* Clinton, Hillary
  Kennedy as role model for, 78–79
  political virtue of, 94–95
  supporters of, 60, 173, 175
  and taxes, 98–101
  and welfare reform, 138
Clinton, Chelsea
  and children's rights, 112–13
  media attacks on, 67–68, 76
  schooling of, 114–15
Clinton, Hillary, 60, 94–115
  charitable causes of, 99, 105
  on children's rights, 103, 110–13
  on corporate America, 103–5, 108
  on education, 113–15
  and environment, 104, 107
  and feminism, 101–2
  gifts claimed by, 97–98
  on greed, 95, 106
  and husband's coattails, 102–3
  investments of, 100, 105–10

Kennedy as role model for, 78–79
law career of, 101–3, 104, 105, 108
memoirs of, 102
moderate views of, 135
political virtue claimed by, 94–96, 115
on Soros, 153
and taxation, 98–101, 216
wealth of, 96–97, 98, 101, 116
and Whitewater, 100, 107–10
Cohen, Randy, 57
Coll, Cynthia Garcia, 211
Colmes, Alan, 5–6
Combs, Sean (P. Diddy), 201
"Company State, The" (Nader), 126
Computer and Communications Industry Association, 128
Congress, U.S., affirmative action practices in, 9–10
Congress Project, 133
Conyers, John, 48
CordeValle Golf Club and Resort, 140–43
Coulter, Ann, 69, 70
Cronkite, Walter, 87
Cuba, Chomsky's visit to, 35–36
Cullman, Lewis and Dorothy, 170

D

Dahrendorf, Sir Ralf, 162
Dailey, Mike, 209
D'Alesandro, "Big Tommy," 136
Damon, Matt, 17
Davis, Tom, 61
D.C. Redevelopment Land Agency, 83–84
Dean, Howard, 4–5
Diller, Phyllis, 117
Dodge, Lowell, 133
Dole, Bob, 62, 76

Donovan, Rick, 104
Douglas, William O., 111
Dowd, Maureen, 4
Downsize This (Moore book), 45, 56
Downy, Dick, 132
Drew, Roy, 106
Druckenmiller, Stanley, 162
Drudge Report, 175
Drug Policy Foundation, 167
Dude, Where's My Country? (Moore book), 45, 49, 53
Du Pont family, 126
Dyson, Michael Eric, 213

E

Early, Gerald, 205
Eastman Kodak Corporation, 22
Edelman, Marian Wright, 106
Edwards, Anne, 179
Eisenhower, Dwight D., 125
Employee Free Choice Act, 149
Environmental Defense Fund, 175

F

Fahrenheit 911 (Moore film), 45, 48, 51
Fallows, James, 133
Family Research Council, 61
Farrakhan, Louis, 201
Federalist Papers, 5
Feinstein, Dianne, 137
Feminist Majority Fund, 175
Fidelity Magellan, 124, 125
Film Society of Lincoln Center, 55
Firestone, 129
Fleet Financial, Boston, 53
Fleischer, Ari, 72
Fletcher, Alphonse, Jr., "Buddy," 206

Hartford Fire Insurance, 129–30
Hastert, Dennis, 140
Hefner, Hugh, 192
Helms, Jesse, 138
Heritage Foundation, 70
Hezbollah, 45
Hill, Doug, 66
Hillsdale College, 4
Hoffman, Nicholas von, 117
Hollywood, racism in, 47–50
Home-Stake Production
   Company, 184
hooks, bell, 8–9
Hoyer, Steny, 139

© Jo Shoupe

ABOUT THE AUTHOR

Peter Schweizer is a fellow at the Hoover Institution and the author of several books, including *Reagan's War* and *The Bushes*. He lives in Florida with his wife and their two children.